David N. Hegarty Author of 'Dynamic Health' and 'Mindful Days.'

Most of the illustrations in this publication are by courtesy of Pixabay, for which I am immensely grateful.

Comments on David Hegarty's work and his previous books:

Sunday Independent; "………'….the secret of good health is much simpler than you think...*Hegarty's no-nonsense approach is a breath of fresh air*....no mystery to good health....people tell him *they never thought it could be so simple*.....**no gimmicks......plain-speaking** advice......*anyone who follows will see a difference, … … …guaranteed.'*

SUNDAY BUSINESS POST.

"A lot of people come and go in the fitness industry, … But someone is now more enthusiastic than he was over 30 years ago, is Dave Hegarty. That's just one of the reasons I admire him…. a purist, as well as being one of the longest established…… conducts his business with integrity…. Hegarty is what the fitness industry is all about"

Liam Griffin, Wexford hotelier, inspirational speaker, renowned business manager, managed the Wexford Senior Hurling team to All Ireland victory in 1996. "… excellent book…. concentrates key foundations to any fitness regime, Posture, Breathing, Relaxation and Diet…. that's what fitness is all about." **Liam Griffin**

Catherine Dowling; founder member and spokesperson of the **Federation of Irish Complementary Therapy Association** " enlightening to read…. very practical…. writing style is easy to read …. *the most sensible programme for mind and body I've come across*"

SUNDAY WORLD

"enhance well-being by making such simple changes. *The programme* for mind and body…………."

Daily Star Ciara Cremin. "At long last, a book full of sense….so easy… …. to keep you fit and healthy and most importantly, give you increased energy…takes a very different approach."

Aslan [rock band] "We were taught to get the best instruments money could buy… But instruments are only as good as the people playing them; that's us.

Or, as we see it, we are the real instruments of our performance. So, we keep ourselves in tune, in key and on song. We practice the simple principles shown in this book. If you read these pages, learn them, and above all, use them … you can bring the music of living into your life."

Publisher's note

Foreword and Dedication.

The significance of good health, in mind and in body, and indeed in spirit, is one of the fastest growing areas of human interest.

And rightly so.

The worth of any nation, continent, country, community, team, or any gathering at all is the worth of the individuals in it.

Being fit, healthy and well is not just about being able to run for the bus, fitting into the jeans, or having a six pack.

We need to be fit for purpose, healthy in mind and body, and well enough emotionally to make the most of who we are, where we are, and with what we've got, for ourselves and for our others.

We all view life differently.

The pieces in this little book have evoked responses from different people for different reasons, but who all had a common aim.

Over the years, indeed over the decades, it has been my privilege to work with people who have shown great courage, strong will, and a persistence in the face of adversity that is nothing short of inspiring.

And perhaps their most endearing and admirable quality was their willingness to apply themselves. And that has been their key to overcoming difficulties, achieving success, or sometimes just surviving; application. Doing.

You may not agree with all of the points raised in this book.

But, on asking yourself why, with an open mind, you may, like others, discover a fresh viewpoint.

This, then, may open doors in the corridor of your mind that will lead you to new discoveries, rooms with views that are new, or you had forgotten about.

I write it with my very best wishes to you for a long, healthy and a happy life,

David Hegarty.

Contents

The Key in The Door of The Cottage...

I paid a visit to a cottage, recently. It had once belonged to my Aunt Maury, who went to live in it 1952. In her mid-fifties then, she'd always looked feeble, and even a bit sickly, with weepy eyes and a querulous tone in her voice. She stood in a kind of hunch, and walked in a shuffle, which emphasized her apparent frailty. Her doctor had vaguely suggested to her that she should take better care of her health, and herself, which she interpreted as being at Death's Door, and so she left Wexford town to live in Kilmore Quay. As far as her mind was concerned she was going to Kilmore to see out the last few days, and if she lasted the journey to there, it was only a matter of moments till she and her life expired, and she, as she put it, 'would be no more nuisance to anyone'.

Despite her appearance, and the frail and helpless impression she perpetrated on the unsuspecting, she had the constitution of an ox, the appetite of a horse, and ate three squares a day that would fuel a fieldworker. She outlived all her contemporaries, and many who were junior to her. When she finally died, she had seen off all those who designated her as a 'blow in', and had established herself as a feature and an icon of the village.

We lived just down the road, and my daily duties, as a robust 8-year-old, were to fetch her daily pail of water, and keep her oil lamps filled, and the wicks trimmed. Running water and electricity were only finding their way, slowly, house by house, into the village.

I used to go to the pump down by the harbour, even though it was farther, and it meant lugging the full pail back up the hill past 'Maddockses' field', and through the village, as far as Maury's. But you'd meet people on the way, or down there, or on the way back, and that meant conversation.

Talking was the social activity those days. Television didn't exist. The only phone in the village was in Paddy and Peg Murphy's Post Office, which doubled as a general store. If you wanted to make a phone call, you went to Paddy. He'd wind the handle, speak to the operator, and then, if he had been successful in getting through to whom you wanted to speak, he'd hand the phone to you, close the door on the phone box, and leave you to it.

There were three radios in the village. We called a radio a 'wireless', and the one with which everyone was familiar was the one in John Sutton's 'Wooden House' pub. The wireless was brought to the premises on Big Match days, when the Rackards and Nick O'Donnell and Ned Wheeler and Art Foley were becoming household names in the county. We had one as well, a 'Murphy', with atmospherics that hissed and crackled and fizzed for a full four or five minutes before the reception cleared, all went quiet, and you could hear what the announcers were saying.

On match days, we'd have a full house, the wireless in the front hall, full volume, and half the village packed up the stairs, in the kitchen, in the dining room, sitting on the outside window ledges, and out into the front garden as far as the road

The front wall was considered a good seat, and the younger men sat there, smoking their Gold Flake and Woodbines, trying to impress the girls with how deeply they inhaled, and how many fags they'd get through during a game.

The harsh and rasping voice of the incomparable Miceál O'Héihir relayed the game, stroke for stroke, reciting the family history of the players as he spoke. 'And now Flynn has the ball, the Garda who's going out with the camogie star May Murphy from the township of Cloyne, whose Aunt Catherine won an All-Ireland medal with the Rebel County when she was only nineteen….and Flynn strikes! …well I can tell you, his sweetheart won't be showering him with affection this evening, when what should have been a green three pointer, has sailed harmlessly wide and let the Slaney-Siders off with a fright and one of Art Foley's long, long puckouts!'

I've forgotten who owned the third wireless in the village.

Matches were spoken of for days afterwards, and with what was read in the papers, what was reported back from those who had attended the games in person, and the wild enthusiasm for which Wexford supporters are known, even today, and the even wilder imaginings as the week went on, it was small wonder that the players became legends.

We had a cinema though. Every two or three weeks, Georgie O'Brien would arrive and entertain us for two consecutive nights.

Georgie travelled the entire South County with his reels and projector, and his arrival in any village was an occasion. We watched for his van, and even though the picture show would have been advertised on posters in Paddy Murphy's and Tommy Howlin's, you could never be sure till you saw Georgie's blue dusty van pull up outside the village hall in the afternoon on the allotted day, that the show, would, in fact, go on.

Back in those days, keys were left in the latch on the doors, especially on the houses where the middle-aged or the elderly lived, so that passers-by would open the door, peer, or walk in, and ask if they could get anything from the shop for the occupier.

The more cautious among the population practised the security of having a piece of looped string hanging from the letterbox. Inside the door, the key was attached to one end of the string, while the other end was tied to a nail or a hook on the back of the door. The caller would then put his hand through the letterbox, extract the key, place it in the lock, and then make his entry.

Maury had this arrangement, and when I went in with a pail of water or messages, or to tend her lamps, I'd give a kind of short yell and announce myself, so that she wouldn't be alarmed.

Though she did have a bit of a problem with hearing, she used it selectively, feigning deafness and ignorance when it suited her. It also allowed her to eavesdrop on the less wary.

I still have one of her oil lamps, the one by which I used to read Robert Louis Stevenson, and the Wexford Free Press, and had started into Charles Dickens, and of course the comics of then, 'The Eagle', and the ubiquitous 'Dandy' and the 'Beano'. I read these to the distant sound of the Atlantic rolling and hissing up on to the Burrow Beach.

Maury died in her nineties, and in her sleep. For many in the village, her passing signalled the end of an era.

And I suppose in some ways, it was. For centuries, the men of Kilmore lived and died by the vagaries of the sea, with few facilities and little in the way of dealing with the storms and high seas that often confined them to the shelter of the harbour. But they're a hardworking and innovative lot, and as the bigger boats and technology became available to them, they put them to very good use.

And a new era arrived. The village grew, and the people in it progressed and learned and made giant strides forward. Their enterprise and willingness have shaped Kilmore into a bustling fishing and tourist port. And that's a good thing.

Kilmore can serve us all as an example of how progress and open minds and willing hearts can transition from era to era, generation to generation, and still retain that link with an illustrious past as the foundation for a splendid and distinguished future.

Some things will never be the same, though.

There are no keys in the doors today.

Duncan Bannatyne's Secret...

'The single most important factor in any company, is the people who work in it.'

Duncan Bannatyne

Everything has a price.

It could be time, it could be money, it could be discomfort, embarrassment, it could be self-denial, humility, even humiliation, or some other kind of self-sacrifice.

But everything worthwhile has some price. And how we think about, feel about, the desired outcome , is usually what determines *how we feel* about the price. If we're wishy-washy in our feelings about our goals, whatever needs to be done can be daunting, even prohibiting.

If we have a very strong desire about the projected outcome, the price may appear small, incidental even.

That's motivation. It works both ways.

To be motivated is to be moved, stirred, inspired, to do something that will cause an effect; it's an emotional response.

We like to see ourselves as mature, rational, logical, clear-thinking adults, unaffected by emotion in our decisions and perceptions, that we live by the intellect and not by the heart. That's mainly because we've been educated to think that that's the ultimate truth.

But it's not.

The term 'Emotional Intelligence' would have been considered almost unacceptable as recently as twenty years ago.

We would have asked how emotion and intelligence could be compatible. Oil and water don't mix. And the use of emotion and the use of intelligence were considered to be mutually exclusive, an oxymoron.

I believe the main reason for this was that the word emotion was associated with a kind of whimsical mindlessness, that to be emotional was ok for soft, irrational, woolly-headed people, people who up to a generation ago were thought to be not of the calibre of the full-blooded, hard-driven, decisive and all-conquering James Bond kind of He-Man. Success in any area of life was generally thought to be the product of Superior Intellect and Brute Force.

Again, not the whole truth.

Women are finally being given the equality they want and deserve. Successful people in any field speak of how they achieved what they did, by the power of how they felt, rather than what they thought.

What they thought about it intellectually may have been in accord with the feeling, *but it would have been the emotion that drove them to action.* Over the past decade, the power of emotion has come to be recognised in any endeavour. And about time too.

Which brings us back to price.

When we're moved, motivated, driven, we're much more likely to persevere in any undertaking. And because of that emotion, that motivation, we're much more likely to come to any task with a will, a drive, a force, whatever the task may be.

In any event in life, anything to which you need to apply yourself, find reasons, when you're starting, why that particular project inspires you. Let yourself think about it, how you feel about it, what it means to you.

Be distinctly personal about it.

Find what it means to *you*, let yourself become come aware of the strength of feeling you have about it, and then, when you've *decided* that that is what you intend, go to it, with a will, and see it through.

Read that again.

If you need confirmation of this, reflect on some event in your life when you went beyond the perceived boundaries, when you searched for, and found, resources you didn't know existed, when you did what you had to do, needed to do, and then saw that event through to its conclusion.

Then, and this is key to the whole process, capture the feeling, the emotion, the sense of drive and energy that pervaded every cell of your existence, and let yourself feel the strength of that feeling again.

Do that daily. And while you're doing it, apply it to whatever you're doing now. Like most people who've done this with a bit of a will, you'll see the difference.

You may find that what you had considered to be a price, was in fact, a privilege

How Strong is Your Desire?.....

'You didn't want it badly enough.'

That was said to a person in a conversation over thirty years ago.

There were about six of us in the group in a bar in Wexford, an old teacher of mine, and five of his ex-pupils, myself included.

I had just had my first book published and that was one of the topics of conversation. One of my pals had said he intended to write a book but hadn't got round to it yet.

Another of the group had made the statement about wanting to do it being the difference.

Even in those days, the number of people starting a full manuscript, getting to the middle, and then completing it was remarkable. In those days, the system was to write your manuscript, have it done, and then send it round publishing houses in the hope that some publisher would go ahead and publish it. Accordingly, to undertake the writing of a complete manuscript was considered a big risk of time and effort, especially if no publisher took it up.

But that was where the difference lay in the desire.

Most people who wrote, did so because of the desire to write, express, put into words what they saw, felt, experienced, imagined, and the aim was to get the writing done, in a story, or some form of non-fiction, so that they had a completed document of their project; getting it published was considered a bonus.

On my first visit to my publisher, Clive Alison's office in Soho, I was amazed to see piles of manuscripts on the window sills, on the stairs, and in calibrated piles in his office; all deliveries from hopefuls like myself.

And his was a considered a small publishing house. But such was the number of manuscripts on his premises, that a conservative estimation of the books being completed every year, and sent in for review to all the publishers in the UK alone, defied calculation.

I happen to know quite a few people who have completed books, written anything from 25,000 words, to 100,000 words, and more. That represents anything from just over 100 pages to up to 400 pages; all on the unsupported hope, and belief, of publication.

But here's my point; once people start to write their work, whatever it may be, they find that they can do it, and get seriously involved in the minutiae as well as the overall process, so that it becomes something of an obsession.

And to take the point further, isn't it wonderful to have that kind of driving purpose? That's the essence of living, where we excel ourselves in effort and energy and application, and all in the name of hope, with absolutely no certainty of publication, let alone getting enough money to live off it.

There are those who'd say that that's daft, others would call it courageous, yet others who's see it as enterprising, but a sad waste of energy, intelligence, and work, that could have been put to something else. Everyone has his own view, and that's fine.

My own attitude would be that I'd hate to get to 95, that's my proposition to Nature, and think, 'Oh damn. I wish I'd done that.'

There was another in our group, a hurler, who had sacrificed what had seemed like a good career opportunity in the USA, to stay in Wexford and vie for his place on the county senior team. He made the panel, played a few games in the jersey, and acquitted himself well.

In a league game in March, he discovered that he would never play to the standard he demanded of himself, that he'd neither the requisite skill, the temperament, nor indeed, the desire to acquire the skill, nor the will to do what was needed to be done if he wanted to keep his place and be a regular county hurler.

He resigned from the panel after the game, and told the gathering that it was a huge relief, a life altering revelation, and a liberating move that opened up a whole new world to him. He has since made a very good career for himself in Public Relations.

C'est la vie.

Desire is a double-edged sword; it can drive us to success, as well as distraction, and to both at the same time.

Wise indeed was the man who counselled, 'Be careful of what you want. You may end up getting it.'

But there is a proviso to that.

So long as desire is harnessed for the good of others and yourself, it can be the force that ignites the fire that blazes the way to a life of purpose, energy, and drive, and a life indeed well lived.

Me, Jake, and The American President.

It's a peculiar thing about life, but we can learn anywhere, at any time, at any age.

Over 65 years ago, in a small seaside fishing village, I first learned a lesson in life that, though I didn't recognize it at the time, was one of the most inspiring and useful pieces of practical wisdom that anyone could wish to experience.

"Take your decision, do it with a will, and see it through."

I was ten years old when I was first told that.

Like most people, I was influenced in life by certain figures.

In times of difficulty, or indecision, or when faced with problems, I often turn to my people of influence for guidance and direction.

Three people figured mainly in my life; an American President, an English Novelist, and Jake.

Jake was a gentle, fearsome, giant of a man. I first met him when I was ten, on a scorching July day, swimming across the harbour. I had paused at his moored boat for a rest, and seeing no one aboard, I had climbed up on the stern deck, where I'd soon fallen asleep in the hot sun.

And that was where he found me, a short time later, when he came to work on his boat.

Jake was highly regarded in the community, not only as a as a fisherman, but even more as a seaman, and highly esteemed as a sailor and a member of the lifeboat crew. He was a quiet, softly spoken individual, except when angered.

In those days, trespassing on property of any kind, usually meant a clip on the ear and being dragged to your parents to explain yourself, or, if you were unlucky, to the local sergeant.

But Jake's approach was different. He started to talk to me about the coiled ropes underneath the deck, tillers, rudders, masts and spars, jibs, mainsails, blocks, halyards, lanyards, beam widths, waterlines, and the thousand and one other things related to small sailing vessels.

For Jake's boat had no engine, you either went with the power of the wind, or got the oars out and put your back into it.

Jake was also reputed to have seven bullets in his body, picked up on a beach in Normandy ten years prior to our meeting, and was rumoured to be living on borrowed time. I never asked about it, and he never offered information, except to say he was on the D-Day invasion, and that was that.

Tragically, the rumour about his borrowed time was true, and Our Jake succumbed to his terrible injuries three years later.

But in those three years, I spent much time with him, hauling lobster pots, laying long lines out around the Saltee Islands, and on the warm windy days in August, chasing the Mackerel up and down Ballyteigue Bay, between Kilmore and Duncannon.

For every day I was privileged to spend with him, he never, ever, let me leave his company without the admonition, "Whatever you do, Boy, take your decision, do it with a will, and see it through."

And so, I learned a lot about maintaining, repairing, running, and sailing, one of the fastest, over-canvassed, best made boats on the South East Coast.

What I didn't realise, was that the man was giving me one of the best life lessons that any boy could get. I only knew that later.

A few years after Jake's passing, in my late teens, and when my adulation for John F Kennedy, the American President, and Howard Spring, the English Novelist, was at its height, I realised that my admiration for both men was because, to my mind, they both fulfilled Jake's criterion for life, 'Take a decision, do it with a will, and see it through.'

JFK had shown his mettle in the Bay of Pigs incident, not to mention taking on Organised Crime with his brother Bobby.

Howard Spring was a perfect role model for any aspiring writer, of any age. He had developed himself in life from very humble and disadvantaged origins, into a journalist, and then a novelist, of the highest calibre.

It was Howard Spring who, for his powers of observation, Churchill brought with him when he went to meet with Stalin and Roosevelt in the Second World War.

Often, in times of difficulty or indecision, I have asked myself what Jake would do in the same circumstances. Whatever the answer, it has always been a help.

And even now, over ᒋ7 years on, when the apprehensions, the doubts, the anxieties, begin to creep in on some project or scheme I'm working on, I hear again that strong, resonant voice, "Take your decision, do it with a will, and see it through."

And so, I do.

Still here. Still listening. Still learning.

Three Proven Ways to Kill Yourself ...

There are a couple of things you need to know, should you wish to complete the job of self-inflicted sickness, depression, lassitude, and eventually, death.

Step One:

Be totally indiscriminate about your food.

Eat any old garbage. Be a rubbish bin.

Guzzle soft drinks, preferably the 'High Energy' ones. Try them with alcohol.

Scoff crisps. Chew chocolate bars at will. Have chips with everything.

Smother them in ketchup.

Make chip sandwiches. These are especially effective at about 11.30 pm, with a gut full of pints. This is your first step into putting your body under siege, and really getting down to the source of sickness, malnutrition and depression.

Do it with a will. Practise it daily. Then you'll get really good at it. It'll become a way of life, your very own self determined life-style, with guaranteed results of withering illness, chronic anxiety, and endless fatigue, and of course, eventual and premature death.

Step Two: Avoid water. This is key.

Water can help the digestive system, keep you hydrated and help eliminate wastes. It's been known to have healthful effects on bodies. Watch it.

Quaff coffee, lattes, cappuccinos, making sure that they're all milked, sugared, and if possible, heavily creamed. Soak them up with muffins, cakes, bikkies or warm scones, heavily buttered, and laden with half a jar of jam.

You can call these snacks. Trivialise them. Pretend you didn't have them. Look on them as little collations that don't count as food, and if anyone asks you whether or not you've eaten during the day, answer, 'Well, I had a little snack or two, but I haven't really eaten.'

This is a great way to ruin your digestive system, confuse your body chemistry, promote severe malnutrition, and set you well on the way to blood sugar levels that will put you into a diabetic stratosphere.

Persist. You're on the way.

Step Three: Make a determined and strong decision to get into alcohol, of any type, kind, or flavour.

Pour it in.

Apply yourself.

As a Race, we've a relationship with alcohol that other countries would consider pathological. Use this advantage to give you a good head start. Recall it often. Embed it in your mind so that nothing will deter you from your aim.

Use the skills you've honed on the food habits to help you get there. Diligence and determination will reward you with a frazzled nervous system, a lot less money, ultimate destitution, and many added effects, like misery, for yourself and those near and dear to you, probable professional disaster, forays into all kinds of interesting little events like bar-fights, crashed cars, humiliation, out-of- control responses and reactions, soiled underwear, shameful behaviour on the street, or at the children's' Confirmation Day, and indeed many other interesting and fun happenings that will add colour to your journey through life.

Don't stop there.

As in all skills, practice is paramount. Get bombed regularly. Box your friends, engage in some spectacular misbehaviour, at work, in the home, your own, or if that's not available as you might be barred from it, anyone else's will do, and of course the old reliable, the restaurant. With perseverance and know-how, you'll soon achieve blackouts, create great enemies, and quickly descend the spiral of failure, despair, and mental disintegration.

You may hit rock bottom before you die.

Watch this.

Resist the urges to reform, get yourself back on track and recover your life.

You'll find any amount of people who could assist you here, but that's the road to sanctuary, convention, and sanity, so take your stand, show your pride, and resist, at all costs, any attempts by these stupid, well-intentioned, busy-body loved ones, or those who profess to be your friends, to give help, assistance, or even love, to your state.

You've worked hard and consistently to get here. You've torn your life apart and successfully destroyed what might have been.

Be strong. Resist. Your aim is total disaster. This is where you dig deep in the reserves and stick with the plan.

Your goal is near.

Just by following these three simple steps alone, you may well find yourself successfully depressed, wonderfully sick, and well on the way to a fulfilled life of misery, unhappiness and massively impressive self-destruction.

One final point. Blame everyone, and everything else. It's all their fault.

That's it. Simple. Proven. Effective. Guaranteed to work.

Or do you have other views on how you'd like your life to be?

We could, for instance, decide that life's ok, that maybe there are a few good things about being alive, that perhaps there are ways, means, available, to use our resources, exploit our abilities, explore and activate our talents. There are those who have taken that view and reportedly enjoy what they experience. They don't always get what they're after, but they apparently get some kind of satisfaction along the way.

I know a lot of people who've tried this. They say it's a good way to live. If you feel that it might appeal, try this:

Check your life-style.

Do a food diary for two weeks.

Observe any drinking or drug use.

Look at your acquaintances, friends, people of influence. Are they good for you? Or not?

Think about your purpose, and whether you're living to help it or hinder it.

If it's out of order, fix it.

Then ask the questions; what can I do about this, how can I do it, when do I do it?

If it's ok, thank whoever your God is, keep it on track, and bear in mind, that there but for fortune, go you or I.

The Use of Choice...

A mirror reflects your image. Water reflects sunlight.

Life reflects.........what?

For most of us, life reflects decisions we've taken.

Who we're with, our jobs, careers, incomes, sense of achievement, or failure, happiness or misery, wealth or poverty, are all largely the result of decisions we've taken somewhere along the way.

Wherever we are, is mostly down to decisions we've taken in the past. And that's good, because if we're happy with the effects those decisions, we can use them again, reinforce the effects.

And if we're not, we can change them.

There is a big difference between brooding over the past, regretting it, and reflecting on the past, and learning from it.

When we're not aware of decisions we've taken which have had unfavourable consequences, there's little we can do about it. Life can continue to be a mysterious calamity.

When we reflect, see a mistake, we can take steps to recovery, redemption, success.

But of course, there are misfortunes that can ambush us; but that's life.

There are no guarantees. But there are aspects of life over which we can exert influence. The influence may not always work exactly the way we hoped it would. But we'll be in a better place than if we let ourselves passively exist in the face of fate, or the object of someone else's plans for us.

Here's a suggestion.

Make an appointment with yourself. In solitude. Meet yourself, and candidly, get that, candidly, write or note or record where you see yourself in your life, and how you think you might either reinforce what you see because you like it, or change what you see because you don't

Robert (Roy) David Hegarty 1929 - 2015

It's just 61 years ago now, 1954. I was ten years old and standing obediently on the steps of Ely Nursing Home, on the shore of the Slaney. My mom was to collect me in the family Vauxhall, a sedate saloon, and bring me home after my very near fatal bout with pleurisy.

She never came.

But a black MG TD, registration number MI 8989, roared through the gate, tore up the driveway and slithered to a halt at the foot of the steps. Out hopped my eldest brother, Roy.

I spread my hands in query, lost for words.

'C'mon', he said.' We're off for a bit of a scooch around the county. It'll blow the cobwebs out.'

'What for?' I asked.

'Celebration' he laughed.

'Celebrating what?'

He walked up the steps, put a hand on my shoulder. 'Your survival, Little Brother. Let's go.'

Back at the car, we climbed over the cutaway doors and plonked on the floor-low seats. Roy fired the engine up and gave a couple of chassis shaking revs. 'Hold on to that' he shouted over the engine noise, pointing to a grabhandle on the passenger side of the dashboard. No seatbelts in those days.

Now, what a grabhandle would do for me, if, rushing through a blind bend, on a twisting Irish country road, accelerating in third gear up to 70 miles an hour, and we ran smack, bang into a Combine Harvester, or a Ferguson tractor, or a cow , or a wandering horse, I don't know.

It was a bit like telling a man in a small boat, caught out in a sudden force 8 gale, to hold on to the mast; you may drown, but you won't go anywhere.

Off we went under a high blue Autumn sky. Turning right at the gate, Roy floored the throttle and we shot off out the Castlebridge road.

To my ten year old eyes, the road streamed open through a shuddering, twisting tunnel of hedgerow. We slowed through the village, Castlebridge, and then picked up again, howling up through Eden Vale, on out through Crossabeg, up and down the hilly country road, wind wild in our hair, the grabhandle holding me on the hopping seat, Roy's hands darting back and forth from the spoked steering wheel to the stubby gearstick, in perfect sync with the singing howl of the straight through exhaust.

Then down the wider concrete road to Ferrycarrig, the MG twitching through the esses underneath the bridge, and accelerating hard up through the steep twists and on out to the Barntown area, where the road levelled and the sturdy, brave, little car settled on the new surface. We sprinted on out to the far side of Clonard.

Taking a sharp right, we barrelled on out through an endless series of totally blind lefts and rights, engine note rising and falling in and out of second and third, on full song, flat out, till we emerged on the New Line, a long straight road, raising and dipping gently through the countryside, all the way back to Wexford town.

Foot to the floor, up through second, the car shot forward. Knocking her into third, roaring on up into fourth, his right foot pressed on the floor, we flattened out along the shuddering, undulating ribbon of road that swept beneath the black, square bouncing bonnet.

The mirror on top of the dash was a shivering blur. I pushed back against the seat, glanced over at the speedo', just touching 95 miles an hour. The MG bounced, skipped, screamed over the hard tarred metalled road. The wind passed straight over us, buffeted up by the aeroscreens.

And then the long, long lefthander, sloping back down to the town, engine slowing, dropping an octave, settling the car at an even steady sixty as we neared the town. On in past the hurling park, slowing all the time, down the road through Bishopswater, ditches and hedges giving way to new housing and streetways as we slowed and rumbled at a crawl of 30 miles an hour, past the Boker, round by Bride St., slowly up John's St., and finally turning into George's St. and home.

I was a bit like one of Bond's cocktails; slightly shaken, much stirred, and imbued with the simmering idea somewhere in the back of my youthful mind that you drive hard, use your gears, perform to the limits of your abilities, but always, always, always, stay between the ditches.

Roy gave me quite a few life lessons, sometimes consciously, sometimes not. From the sliding seat on a planning Hornet dinghy, I learned that sometimes you stayed the course, but when it blows up hard, never be afraid to run for cover.

I had great kindness from him and Eithne, and Maggs and Pete and Rob.

And it was very good to know too that he experienced the same in his final years from his own family and from Anton and Liz and Mark and Joyce.

Francoise and I met him a couple of years ago in Dublin, not long after Eithne's passing. I thought a large part of him had gone with her. He told me he'd had a good life, no complaints. I believe as well that he made a strong, positive impression on those he knew.

So let's not only mourn his passing, but celebrate too, a life well- lived, well-marked, and well-remembered.

Rest in Peace.

POWER...

An emotive word, 'power'. It conjures up all kinds of images, depending on our own outlook and experience of the world.

To many, it suggests the tyrant cutting a swathe through some form of defencelessness. But that's just the standard image of the 'baddie', exemplifying the abuse of power. Power is more than that. It's an ability to influence, persuade, cause desired effects that can be good, to take place.

And there's a power for everyone.

Most of us underestimate the availability of it and eschew the use of it.

The power of decision is for all.

Anyone, anywhere, anytime, can seek, and take, a decision that will change lives, alter circumstances, make life a worthwhile pursuit of happiness.

And that's our own individual privilege and decision in life. We can take a decision tomorrow that we're going to do (your own thing)...................... And then go and do it.

Or try to. The very decision will give life meaning, direction, purpose.

It doesn't have to be one of the conventional goals; it can be anything. Anything at all. Something that means a lot to you, or me, or yer man. It's your own business. But it's what makes a difference between existing and living.

In the speed and relentlessness of life today, we tend to lose touch with ourselves. We're busy keeping up, staying the pace, surviving. We can't open our eyes or ears without a barrage of news, event, outrage, or other calamity distracting us.

We react, as humans do, in kind. We become nervously aware of pending misfortune, possible disasters, imminent setbacks. Life, *unless we take a decision*, can take over and condition us out of existence.

And that's why we have an intelligence; to put it to use. But that takes a conscious decision.

Now, that doesn't mean we solve all our problems overnight. But it does mean we're reasserting our initiative.

And that's for everyone.

'Little Fat Paddy'

A conversation, just a week or so ago, with a good friend, had a strong after-effect. It was a bit like the earthquake that demolishes a landmass after it has occurred.

He had spoken about his need to be motivated, moved, impelled, to take a particular course of action.

'I do fine for a few days,' he said, 'Then I fall off and undo the good work I've achieved up to then. The thing is that I know what to do, how to do it, even get into it, with great drive and energy, and then the inspiration goes, and the good intentions, and I'm back where I started.'

And then he added a phrase that resonated with an experience of my own.

He said, 'The thing is, when I find myself back in square one, *I find I don't really care.'*

His astute observation struck a loud chord. It reminded me of an incident which I'd related to a couple of people some time ago.

It's about motivation, how it affects us, where it can come from, the disguises in which it can be hidden.

This took place over 56 years ago. I was 21, living on the Kentish border, just outside London.

I was training regularly, fit, active, had good energy.

But I wasn't that well. I'd bloated to fourteen and a half stone, existed on a high fat, high sugary diet, supplemented with the usual week-end excesses of what 21-year-olds got up to in my day.

But I'd always had the belief in, and fidelity to, the discipline of physical exercise and the practice of breathwork.

But the exercising was becoming hard work, slower, more ponderous, even uncomfortable. The body, and of course the mind, were in a different mode than that with which I normally performed.

I heard the warnings from a great friend and mentor, Peter, of that time; heart, arteries, organs, attitude, would all be affected, he told me.

My youthful hubris dismissed his kind advice as that of an alarmist; I could eat, drink and be as merry as I wanted. Or so I thought.

He took another angle. He said I looked fat, podgy, that my shirts were bursting and my three chins gave a pretty sad kind of profile. He said he'd heard me described as a slob, a fit slob, but nonetheless, a slob.

I replied, 'If anyone doesn't like what he sees, he needn't ****ing well look!', and that, I figured, nailed that.

Or, again, so I thought.

What happened a couple of weeks later changed everything.

Two pals and myself had booked a day at Brands Hatch, the racing circuit, for the opportunity to drive souped-up saloons and a formula car.

We went down in my old 1946 Rover 10, which I'd bought for £12.00. We cruised at what was considered a racy 55 miles an hour.

When we arrived, the three of us, and a group of about 9 others, were greeted and brought into a room to be briefed on the skills and etiquette of circuit driving as learners. We ranged in age from about seventeen to what appeared to me to be about a hundred and ninety.

We were then brought out, given a helmet each, and put in an assortment of stripped and tuned Anglias, Humber Sceptres, and Austin A35's. Then we lined up behind Tony, the instructor, and were led for 5 lively and exhilarating laps as we followed his line, got used to the cars, and began to get the hang of the event.

Then we had another briefing, and off we went again, this time a bit more quickly, with deeper braking points, a few line changes, and everything happening more quickly. We were getting accustomed to the circuit, the noise, the constant gear changing, and the proximity of the other cars. It was hard physical work, and the concentration was intense.

During a break after that stint, we sat on the grass and drank hot, sweet tea, which was very welcome. I was hot, sweaty and a bit overwhelmed by the whole experience. The conversation among all of us was surprisingly quiet, thoughtful, recounting our individual experiences with care, mindful of what we were saying.

I think that we felt we were on some kind of journey, that it was leading to some revelation in our lives. I know that my own impression was that this was not as easy as it looked, and my regard for people who did it seriously soared into the stratosphere.

We discovered that none in the whole group had ever driven on a circuit, or in a highly tuned car. Then Tony gathered us into a huge trailer and told us that the next part was to drive in Formula Junior Racing cars. He complimented us on having listened to his previous instructions and said that if we paid the same attention to the next bit, that we'd discover a lot, and bring the experience to another level.

We listened respectfully. Then we togged on the helmets again and were led off to the racing cars. We got into the cars, and based on observations, I was third in line. Then we lined out behind him, onto the track, and followed as before.

The sensation of a purpose-built racing car, with the open wheels, in full view, the instant response to the right foot, the light steering, the short gearchange, and the driving of it, at what seems ten time faster than you ever imagined, gives a sense of control that is itself tremendously fulfilling.

The noise is incredible. As the power of the front engine shudders through the machine and yourself, you're aware that you're playing a mechanical instrument. You become immersed in the process of placing the wheels and the car for a bend, instinctively dropping a gear, easing power on as you cross the apex, letting the screaming vehicle move across the bend and out on to the far margin, then straightening up and snatching back into the next gear again.

Exhilarating is an understatement.

We finished the five energising, exhausting, laps, had another briefing, and a change in line-up. One of the elderly gentlemen was brought up to my place, and to my surprise, I was shifted to the front.

The atmosphere of the meeting was quietly intensive, almost physical.

Then out we went again, following Tony in a rumbling, noisy, orderly line.

The first lap was easy enough, following lines, hitting brake points, revising the circuit.

The second the third laps were a bit quicker; the bends were coming more quickly, gear changing was setting into a rhythm, the car was more responsive, the steering lighter, a pattern was emerging.

Lap four was a transformation. The car was coming alive. The roadway was a guiding surface with the practiced moves and lessons all falling into place.

The engine note had raised an octave, responding, changing, shifting the car through the turns, bellowing in a high scream on the short straight bursts, all in a steady controlled tempo.

We passed two of the other participants on the start of lap five. Then, braking for the hairpin at Druids, we slipped past two more. The feeling was euphoric. But then, accelerating hard out of that bend, setting up for the fast lefthander out onto the short bottom straight, something happened.

The spell broke. It all fell apart.

The concentration, the pace, the effortless rhythm, just vanished.

Suddenly, I was aware of the unfamiliar speed, the overpowering noise, the alarming nearness of the other cars, how close we were to the edge, and a dreadful sense of danger. And my own vulnerability.

The remainder of that lap was a lumpy, disjointed, uneven scramble back to the finish line, with an overwhelming relief when we came to a halt.

As if in response to the disintegration of that last half lap, I heaved my sweating, exhausted and heavy body from the cockpit. I took off the helmet and walked to Tony to return it.

He was looking at me oddly. 'Don't worry,' he said, 'It happens everyone'

'What does?' I asked.

'Brain fade. I saw it in the mirror after you left the hairpin.' Then he added with a kindly smile. 'I wondered how long you'd stay at that pace. For a first timer, that was good, especially the fourth lap; neat, quick, smooth. Not bad at all', he grinned, ' Nice driving'.

I thanked him, shook his hand, and was about three paces away from him when I heard him utter to one of his mates, 'That Little Fat Paddy can drive.'

Nothing unkind. No malice in it. He was simply describing what he was seeing.

Little Fat Paddy.

I was elated. And I was mortified.

Elation came from the recognition, the acknowledgement, from a professional, that I had some kind of aptitude for driving. Deep embarrassment came from my own recognition that what he said was true. There was nothing unfair or inaccurate about it. He described what I presented to the outside world.

No doubt, the terms wouldn't be used or accepted today, but in those days, such terminology was freely expressed. What made the difference was the tone.

The truth was that the image I presented was truthfully depicted by the man's words.

And I realised something as the picture hit home; I did care.

Later, I took a good look, an honest look, at myself.

Physically and mentally, I'd deteriorated. Though I trained and exercised, it was superficial

The purpose had gone. I'd become automaton, going through the motions, aimless, without substance. I felt I was living a lie, paying lip service to the beliefs and ideals I'd once held, practicing a self-delusional infidelity. Dreams had faded, disappearing into a morass of indifference, and the strong sense of personal purpose had all but vanished.

But not quite.

Somewhere in the deepest recesses glowed an ember. And all that ember needed was a spark, a draught, to brighten the glow, ignite the fire, fan the flame. And that statement, casually uttered, thrown out by the speaker, unintended for my ears, was the spark.

'Little Fat Paddy.'

I'd been abashed at the words the man had used to describe me, not because he'd said them, but because of their truth.

There was no one to blame but myself. I had put myself there.

And so, it was, that I realised, with a warm swell of gratitude, that I could therefore get myself out of there. I took courage and energy from the fact that I had the wit to see it. And that I knew what to do, and how to go about it.

Almost to the day, twelve weeks later, I drove down to Brands again. This time I was on my own. The visit had a purpose.

Along with other projects that had been undertaken and achieved in that short twelve weeks, my lovely old Rover gleamed in the Autumn sunshine. She'd been serviced, tuned and lovingly prepared to represent the classic that she was. The body was good, the chassis sound, the internals in good working order. The car hummed.

And I'd done a bit of work on myself as well.

Back down to my eleven stone two pounds, I had got myself fit, lean, energetic and well. I parked the car and went to sign on for the day's driving. Tony wasn't there. But that didn't matter. This visit wasn't about the driving.

There was an agenda to the journey. Twelve weeks had been the time I'd set myself to refute and annihilate, what had been to me, a self-made threat to my very existence.

I'd told myself I'd go back down to Brands Hatch, that I'd be at my good weight, and in good condition; and that had been my goal. So, I was able to spend an enjoyable day, in pleasant company.

Later, leaving the circuit, I was aware of a vastly different feeling from the previous visit.

The Rover, and myself, felt restored, well-tuned, and reliable. With a quiet sense of accomplishment, and a richly deep gratitude, we hummed back up the road towards London, to new a beginning, and the next step.

That summer had been an enlightening and educational experience. And a lasting one. As an easy weight gainer, I need to discipline myself to keep in good condition. But I've a great motivator; to this day, the letters LFP stand sentinel on my fridge door, a clear and unequivocal reminder of what I once promised myself, fifty-six years ago.

It reminds me that life is not so much about what happens to us, but what we're prepared to do about what happens to us.

Mission Statement...

Are we bringing business methods into the realm of personal living?

Could be. If it works, use it. And isn't business an expression of personal aspiration anyway?

So, as one coach in the UK emphasizes, maybe it's time we acknowledged the importance of *being personal* in business affairs.

There has always been, over the decades, a distinction, with which I disagree strongly, that business is a separate entity to the people in it. 'Nothing personal', goes the phrase, 'It's just business.'

The impression given is that people interfere with the mechanics of a system, as in franchising. And there is a point to which that applies; the system needs to be adhered to and applied with a consistency that allows it be effective.

But, but, but.........

The consistency of the system is only as good as the people who apply it, and how they apply it, and the vigour, the drive, the belief, the enthusiasm, with which they apply it.

So, back to the people and the members of the team; the fielders need to be able to catch the ball, then pass it to the game makers, who feed the goal scorers, who stack up the points.

The analogy stands for any group of two or more people in any engagement.

So, what's this to do with mission statements?

Here's what.

Two weeks ago, I was suggesting to a person to consider a Statement of Intent, a morning statement in which he set a direction and intention for the day. He dismissed it as 'woo-woo codswallop', when I asked him if he had a mission statement for his company. Which he did, and which he quoted verbatim with great force and eloquence.

He'd barely finished his quotation, when he laughed. 'Yeah', he said, 'I get it.'

Nourishment of the mind is a simple process. A bit like the computer, what we put in, we tend to get out. Obviously, with humans, it's a bit more sophisticated and subtle than that; but it's still a sound principle.

A mind that's set to the aims of a mission statement, fuelled with the human elements of drive and energy, can aspire to more creative, productive, accomplished aims than a mind left to the whims and distractions of daily life could ever even begin to contemplate.

Nourishment. Of the mind. A skill.

A practice, once embarked on, that develops its own force and revelation, that staggers the imagination.

Read that again, right now. Think on it for a day or so. You'll get a nifty little directive in the next posting.

Shape Your Day, Change Your Life...

"One day at a time" is applicable to more than staying off drink. We live life one day at a time. Most of our troubles come from trying to live last month, next month, next year, three years' time, in the day in which we really need to be living, the one we're in now.

What's gone is gone. We can't change it, better it, alter it. We can learn from it, relegate it to the past and get on with the rest of our lives.

In the sixties, some fellow in Madison Avenue came up with the phrase, "Tomorrow is the first day of the rest of your life", which I thought was a useful observation, as it gave meaning to the activities, the decisions of today, all of which influence where we'll be tomorrow.

It made sense of the idea of living a day at a time, which isn't just for recovering alcoholics.

That said then, we 're all agreed that what we do today, how we apply ourselves today, how we respond to what's going on in our lives today, will contribute to where we are tomorrow. So then, it makes perfect sense, doesn't it, to make the most of who we are, what we do, take initiative for today, as that'll influence tomorrow, and tomorrow will influence the next day, and that day will influence the one after that, and all the other tomorrows.

That works both ways. People who have addiction problems started with the first drink, the first shoot-up, the first bet on a horse or a dog, and then followed on with it on the next day. And the next.

Habits are mental. They're patterns of thought that direct our minds, our subsequent thoughts, and HOW we're thinking, that then affects how we feel, and that's what directs our actions, behaviour, performance, reactions, in fact, how we live.

They can be directed. Sometimes it's pretty quick, sometimes not so.

But when we take a decision to start any given day in our lives with a directive, whether we achieve it or not, we've taken the first step.

Awareness takes place. We may not achieve the overnight success we feel we deserve, but we're getting there. Persistence is the key. Persistence is about getting up again, back on the horse, not capitulating, not giving up.

So, Back to today. That's the start. Simple.

Here's a suggestion; start your day with a thought. Not any old thought that falls into your mind from the radio or wherever, but with a thought that appeals to you as an ideal, or a goal, or an aspiration for your life, or some event or person in your life that means a lot to you in a vibrant, positive, enjoyable way.

Now put that thought into words.

Verbalise it in language that appeals to *you*. Keep it to yourself at this stage. It's a personal, private kind of thing, and you'll be comfortable with it so long as you're not having to worry about who thinks what of it. And anyway, it's not for anyone else's opinion or approval; it's your idea and it's your business.

And here's another suggestion, one which a lot of people find very helpful. Prepare it and have it in your mind, the night before, that you're going to start the next day with that thought, in words, that have a meaning for you.

Do that, every night and every morning.

Our lives are a series of mornings and nights, so when we institute a pattern at a given time, every morning, and every night, we simply create and reinforce that pattern of thought into our lives and allow it form the habits of thinking which subsequently emerge.

And before you dismiss this as some simplistic waste of time, consider the mission statement of a company, the principle that directs every decision, policy and procedure of an organisation; it is usually learned, memorised and quoted around the company on a frequent and forceful basis. And if it isn't, it should be. The mission statement is the company mantra, to be learned, internalised and lived.

This is simply your personal mission statement, your own personal mantra.

Tricks of The Mind...

When did you last decide to be fitter, leaner, healthier, more well, less stressed, in good shape, or condition?

And then did it?

It's not the easiest thing to do, not because of physical, financial, social, professional, or other constraints, but more often because we cop out.

We talk ourselves out of it. We listen to the inner voices, the ones that tell us it's ok to leave it till tomorrow, do it another day, don't worry about it now, it'll all work itself out.

And of course, it doesn't. Nothing works itself out.

Anything and everything happens as the result of a cause. Getting an aim accomplished in any aspect of life is the result of applying specific actions, applying causes that create effects.

When we get a fright about our health, we find it very easy to quit smoking, reduce the drink, take exercise.

Sometimes, though, we can leave it too late, and by the time we take a decision to do something, the damage has been done, the consequences suffered.

So, how do we get ourselves in the frame of mind to manage our health?

We start with a decision. We take time out. Think about it, mull over it, contemplate it. That might take ten minutes. Or ten days. It doesn't matter.

Then we decide.

Decision is vital.

Conscious, considered, personal decision is what makes the difference to any cause. And that's what life is, isn't it, a series of decisions?

Look at the numbers who descend on the gyms in January and February, then disappear in March.

The ones who stay are those who joined because of a considered decision, not because it's the thing to do in January.

For a decision to hold water, it needs a reason.

WHY would you want to achieve a wellness? Get a bit fitter? Get rid of flab?

Take time on this.

Consider why you'd want any of those goals. And make the REASON yours. It doesn't need to conform to some socially acceptable purpose. Or to someone else's opinion, or approval, or requirement.

Find YOUR reason. And don't worry if it changes. Keep exploring. You may find that you'll give yourself all sorts of nicely sounding ones, and then finally come up with something like 'I'm fed up with my big belly,' or 'my fat arse', or 'squeezing into my jeans'.

It doesn't matter what it is, so long as *it drives you* to take a decision, a real decision, not some wishy-washy notion that has all the force of a fart on the ocean.

Go to it. Pen and paper, or your keypad, whatever.

But start there. That's the source and the substance; a sound decision and a personally felt reason to want to do it.

Good luck.

80% Mental, 20% Mechanical...

Every day, science seems to be confirming what we've believed all along; that we've a lot more influence on our health, wellness, longevity, than we think.

The World Health Organization blames malnutrition for 75% of the illness in the world. And they're not talking about starvation in third world countries. A lot of the population in the wealthier parts of the Western world suffer from malnutrition. This was borne out by research done by the authors of the book 'Food Fight', by Kelly Brownell and Catherine Horgen.

The world is becoming conditioned to the use of processed food, with poor nutrition, high fat, and high sugar content.

Our food today is nicely packaged, chemically enhanced, to give texture and taste, and either ready to cook, or even precooked.

We now see it as the normal food to eat. Our minds have been steered to accept it with clever advertising, celebrity endorsement, and the convenience it offers in our hectic modern lives.

Much the same can be said for how we think about exercise. Bristol University offers evidence of 80% of the population not even meeting the government recommended exercise levels; 12 half hour sessions of activity per month.

Our minds are still very much in the way of taking for granted the health, energy, vitality that we have.

And we need to change that. It doesn't mean doing 6 miles a morning, seven days a week, or living on nuts, bananas and multivitamins.

But it does mean developing a system; training the mind, creating a pattern, that serves us well in the food and exercise areas.

And that's the first place, the mind.

That's where we make the decisions, the good and the bad.

We start there and work from that point.

Five Things to Do for Good Nourishment...

Here are five things to do which will make sure you get the right kind of food into your system to keep you healthy, well and strong.

1.   Plan what you're going to have for the week ahead. You may or may not stick rigidly to it, but it'll be in your mind and will influence decisions you would otherwise fall into unconsciously.

It helps prevent the ambushing we perpetrate on ourselves all day long. That's the power of Mindful Awareness.

2.   Allocate a time, and even a place, for your eating. It makes a ritual and strong association of the habit. This gives it a direction which is more compatible with your purpose.

3.   I know you've all heard this before, but here it is again; CHEW. MASTICATE. Make the food into mulch by the time it's delivered to your poor unsuspecting stomach. The best diet in the world is rendered practically useless if the digestive system is under siege.

4.   Be selective and persistent in your choice. No one else has an opinion that is more important to you, and more

personal to you, and more under your conscious influence, than your health. Be true to yourself and your aims. They're your affair and your responsibility. Stick up for them. Be loyal to them.

5. We all have the power of decision. And it's ours, and ours alone, to use. Where you are next week, next month, next year, depends on what decision you make today.

Today is vital. What we decide today, steers our lives and opportunities and ultimate results and what they become.

Today is critical.

Overfed, Undernourished......

The irony of the incredible progress that the world has made is that while our *standards* in living seem to be improving, our *quality* of life may be diminishing.

Maybe we need some Darwinian evolutionary techniques in our arsenal of adaptation.

One of the huge contradictions of today is how we use our food. Maybe a good idea is to ask ourselves why we eat in the first place.

For enjoyment? Sure, why not?

Because it's dinnertime or lunch-time? Many do.

Because we're hungry? Certainly, and the best reason so far.

The real reason we've a hunger trigger is that we need certain elements supplied by food to grow, repair and maintain the cells of the body. And the one single nutrient that allows this take place is protein.

We get this from the fish, meat, poultry and the eggs that go to make up most of the dinners and lunches in the country today.

We can get it from cheese and other dairy too, milk and derivatives, but the human digestive system is generally best served by well-chewed examples of the former.

It is now generally accepted that the human body needs in or around 100 grams of protein every day.

Most of the meals we eat daily are lower in protein than is recommended, so we need to be aware and practising the art of putting protein-rich foods into our daily eating habits.

While we also need a small amount of sugars in caring for the cells of our bodies, we get all we need from vegetables and fruit.

What we don't need is the amount of sugar we get from the manufactured foods that populate the shop shelves today.

Vitamins, minerals, trace elements, we should be getting from fruit and vegetables as well.

But by the time we've put the insecticides, pesticides, stored and cooked and prepared the plants or the fruit, there's little or none of these to speak of.

The answer is to take a reliable vitamin supplement.

The other factor that we need to address is the huge amount of sugar we're ingesting. For years, when I suggested to people to reduce the amount of sugars and starches in their diet, I was told that their diet was fine because it was all 'low fat'. Which is what the Americans were on too, and we all know the state of obesity in America.

Here's your first step to a long and healthy life; cut your sugars right down, especially the man-made ones. Use your natural sources. Get an adequate protein content into your meals.

In other words, if it walks, flies, swims, or grows, eat it.

Cut right back, or out altogether, boxes, tins, and other packaged food.

Simple as it seems, it'll change entirely the quality of your food, the effects on the cells of your body, the way you feel, think, look and live.

Start there.

The Greatest Quality

"Nothing in the world can take the place of persistence.

Talent will not; nothing is more common than unsuccessful men with talent.

Genius will not; unrewarded genius is almost a proverb.

Education will not; the world is full of educated derelicts.

Persistence and determination alone are omnipotent."

1872-1933, Thirtieth President of the USA, Coolidge, Calvin

Have We Got this Right...?

When asked: *"What surprises you most about humanity?"* the Dalai Lama answered:

"Man. Because he sacrifices his health to make money.

Then he sacrifices money to recuperate his health.

And then he is so anxious about the future that he does not enjoy the present.

Because of this, he does not live in the present or the future.

He lives as if he is never going to die, and then dies, never really having lived."

"I never could have done what I have done without the habits of punctuality, order, and diligence, without the determination to concentrate myself on one subject at a time."

Charles Dickens

1812-1870, Writer

Do You Do This...?

Succeeding at something is a bit like exercising. You know it's good for you, you feel very good about it, and yourself, when it's done. But it can be an easy thing to avoid.

Good results came to a man recently who decided to apply himself routinely to the habit of breathwork.

That was his first step; taking the decision. Now it wasn't a wishy-washy vague kind of hope that he might get around to doing it. He started with a real decision. He decided to commit to it for six weeks, see where it took him, and go from there. But the six weeks and the decision were sacrosanct.

He blocked off time in his phone calendar. He put memos in his appointment book to remind him to use this truly useful technique to set himself up for meetings. He wanted to be in the right frame of mind, the mindset that would help him. He wanted to ground himself, be aware of the purpose of his meetings.

He set times of the day to devote to this practice of stilling the mind, settling the nervous system, calming his emotions.

He made appointments with himself to get it done.

And he honoured those appointments as he would any other business meeting. He gave it the seriousness that held him to his self-agreement. And he got it done. And of course, he felt better, performed better, and got better results.

It brings order, pace, equilibrium, into what can so easily fall into chaos.

Whatever goes on in our lives, we have a choice, somewhere along the line, to exert an influence on it; a good and useful influence.

Breathwork, well done, with a bit of mindfulness and will, renews and reconstructs lives on a daily basis.

For the people who do it.

Is This a Good Idea...? Really..?

Everything starts with an idea. Everything.

And yet, ideas are often discarded at the first sign of difficulty as if they were only a wistful thought, a dreamy insubstantial flit of the imagination that really didn't have the substance to be considered further.

And that's a pity. Some people have wonderful ideas, but they need thought and serious consideration in order to be brought to fruition.

For centuries, Man tried to fly, jumping off cliffs, strapping himself to wings and flapping furiously, hilariously even, tying ailerons to bicycles and pedalling frantically in the hope of defying the gravity that just wouldn't let go.

And while we all laugh and amuse ourselves at their antics, we need to remind ourselves that their ideas were fine; they just didn't have the technology to advance them.

Now we sit in a winged tube and go anywhere in the world for the price of a ticket.

But it all started with an idea, a belief, that there was a way to make it happen.

Ideas are priceless. Some ideas have no precedent, and when they're expressed, get dismissed because the listeners don't see what the speaker does. That's when the ideas man must hold his vision, keep the thought, have the courage of his conviction.

It's good to remember too, that the man who never had a bad idea, rarely had a good one either.

Starting a business, finishing a business, changing a business, or a job, or a husband, or a wife, or taking a chance on some apparently looney project, are all products of an underlying idea.

Ideas grow. When an idea can grow, to get researched, thought about, developed, usually one of two things happens; the idea gets shelved, or it gets produced.

Or the thoughtfulness can lead to something else, a variation of the idea, or the discovery of another idea that turns out spectacularly successful.

Any one in business will tell you of how they once went to try something, and though it may not have worked out as they thought it would, has contributed to another aspect of their lives.

A client of mine applies an analytical approach to most things he does. While he was creating a schedule for his own workouts, and specially for his rounds of meditation, and his dietary needs, he found it worked very well; it gave consistency to his practice.

He then applied the same principle of scheduling to his staff meetings, staff training programmes, and his marketing strategies, and used progress in his business as a measurement of his efforts.

Over a three-month period, there was a big improvement in all aspects of his affairs, not the least of which was a happier ship, as the crew now had regular and systematic ways to check, rehearse and apply their strategies.

All from an idea.

Ideas are the vessels in which we probe the frontiers of our imagination. We carry our hearts and minds to new places. We challenge and develop our courage and self-belief.

Ideas are an area of privilege, where the human being can extend himself and explore the horizons of what's possible.

They can bring the power of really living to any life.

Which is a nice kind of idea, isn't it?

Simple Success...

We're all well agreed, I believe, that doing the simple things, very well, daily, is what usually ensures success.

In any endeavour.

We also know that the most significant thing in any undertaking is putting it into action; no action, no results.

A man said to me recently that he never thought it'd be so easy to achieve a target he'd set for himself.

The interesting thing was that he'd been thinking about it for years. And he'd made one or two half-hearted stabs at it. Which gave him half-hearted, dispiriting results.

Then he took a decision, said he was going to do whatever it took, and started.

The results fairly jumped at him. And as quickly as that. Which is not at all surprising, because we know that if we take a decision, a firm, solid decision, we'll do what we need to do, and the results will come.

So, for this month, look for something you've been threatening to do for a while. Then take a decision to START it.

And do that little, or big, bit every day. Every day. Do five minutes or five hours. But start the process.

And just do it every day. It may take you a month, or a year, or a day, to get it into swing and to make progress, but you'll have started it and it'll become something you're doing, not talking about, thinking about, wondering about.

It'll grow in your mind and in your life because you're giving it the nourishment of activity, which will fuel your belief and imagination. It'll soon begin to take on the form of being real.

Ask anyone who's written a book, started a business, made a change in their career. When you start something, you bring it into the realm of possibility. That's the first step.

Start.

The Fear and the Doubt...

Here's a delightful and inspirational piece of verse that someone recited to me recently, and real fuel for the day;

Seek not to banish Fear or Doubt

In the outside Noise and Din.

The Peace you're seeking from Without,

Comes only from Within

The Power of Practice...

Being fit and well is simply achieved. You don't have to break your back, push yourself beyond your limits, or go beyond 'pain barriers'.

The system is a process, not an event.

Once the fundamentals are learned, you practise them.

'Practice makes perfect', is an old cliche, but nonetheless true for that. When you practise the fitness principles, you get good at them. And then better. Just as you would if you played piano, rode a horse, or drove a car. After a while, you don't have to think of WHAT you're doing, which allows you concentrate on HOW you're doing it.

That's what makes the difference to the results you get.

So, the first aim is to learn **what** to do, then **how**, then you **do it**.

You make minor alterations, small improvements, little switches.

And they all add up to a huge difference.

It's good mental discipline, a mental exercise, a neuro-muscular skill.

The focusing on the positive activity in search of a positive outcome, creates a positive state of expectation

On a Beach in Normandy...

On a recent visit to France, I did something I'd been meaning to do for over 40 years, and spent a day visiting some of the beaches in Normandy. These are the beaches in Northern France on to which 175,000 troops scrambled and fought and stormed, many of them never to return, in the Second World War, on D-Day, June 6th., 1944.

A day isn't long enough to spend there.

Four hours at one beach alone, just begins to impact on the mind and the imagination the enormity of the event, the triumph and the tragedy of it, the genius and intellectual application in the planning, the logistics involved, the chaos and the spectacle of the event itself, and the price in human suffering of the consequences of war.

Having seen movies, read books, listened to documentaries on the D-Day landings, I imagined I'd have some idea of what to expect.

Well, nothing, nothing, prepares you for the reality of standing on a patch of sand beside a gun-emplacement, a three-meter-thick concrete bunker, just one hundred yards from the water's edge, feeling the wind, hearing the seas rolling in, and realizing that that tiny piece of geographical fixture is almost exactly as it was on that day, seventy-three years ago.

The reality of it is a shock.

Before going out on the beach, I'd been primed, in the Canadian Memorial Centre overlooking the sea, with stories, pictures, statistics, that then translated into a sense of presence, so that the walk to, and on, the beach was something akin to a spiritual experience. It wavered between being wondrous and being eerie.

We were a small gathering. As we moved out to the beach, there was a mixed sense of apprehension and anticipation in the group. I was also aware that we were regarding each other. Some kind of an effect was taking place.

The sound of the waves, the gusting North-East wind, the barren and empty strand, the cry of the odd overhead gull, all served to fire the mind with the noise that the guide was describing, the shouts of officers, rattling machine guns, strafing, howling, dive-bombing planes, naval bombardment, exploding shells, rumbling tanks.

And of course, screaming men.

I'd been speaking in the Centre with Ben, a Canadian, and a nephew of a D-Day combatant. Ben was about six-four, a gregarious, pleasantly mannered man, knowledgeable of the invasion, and informative. He was also a Vietnam veteran, and this trip was a kind of personal pilgrimage to the place where his beloved uncle had stormed and died, all those years ago.

Myself and another, a Londoner, who had three uncles who survived the beaches and the aftermath, and had lived to ripe old ages, tagged on to Ben and we walked with him.

The big Canadian discreetly added odd bits of detail to the guide's narrative, giving us the benefit of much more than just a guided tour. Snippets of individual doings personalised the entire happening, imbuing it with the pathos and hue of helpless humanity.

We moved along, getting the story of the physical landing, on the spot where it happened, where the water ran red, where moments and deeds of hope became instant death, where the land and the sea and the sky was a chaos of turmoil, death and destruction. As the guide threw out facts and statistics that gave truth and reality to her harrowing description, I realized I wasn't beside Ben any more.

And he wasn't with the group.

I turned and searched, and there he was, on his own, about twenty feet away, a forlorn and lonely figure, in his incongruously bright red jacket, and his inappropriately jaunty baseball cap, his large frame shuddering in sobs as no doubt he connected with his dead uncle in a way that inexperienced mere observers like myself could never begin to imagine.

We moved on then. Ben re-joined us at the tail end of the small group, very calm and quiet, in a different place. And apparently, at peace.

I certainly hope so.

We walked on in the path of the youthful Canadian guide, as she proudly walked the way of some of her ancestors. She spoke with energy and certitude, with a strong sense of respect and pride, in her tone and in her gait, experiencing the privilege of her own performance.

As with many human experiences, the effect is often greater on reflection, when the fact of the matter has had the time to sink in, and we ponder on things like accidents of birth, which put those men there at that time, and not us, and what some of those who died on those beaches might think of the world as it is today.

They'd probably echo the words of the song that asks, 'When will we ever learn?'

Take a Breather...

We live in troubled times. And we live at a rate for which we weren't designed.

Evolution is lagging a bit in helping us adapt.

So, we need to do what we can to preserve the integrity of our minds and bodies and souls in a life that's threatening to outpace us.

We need to see the value of rest, being able to stop, come to a halt, still the mind.

That's Mindful Awareness.

(The word 'Mindful' is becoming a bit like the word 'Beautiful' in the sixties; nearly everything that wasn't terrible was described as beautiful. Now when some people find themselves skiving and doing nothing they describe it as 'being Mindful'.)

Which is ok if it keeps the mind in tune, on set, with the attitude.

Mindful Awareness can be a powerful way to bring pace, rhythm, a set tempo, into our lives. It makes for calmer living, reserved energy, and a sense of direction and personal purpose.

It gives us time to reflect, to take considered decisions about everything from resisting the doughnut to changing our careers.

We tend more to look at the world from the inside out, to consider how we can best use ourselves in the walk of life, to our own and others' benefit.

Think on it.

So, What's Yours...?

During the time of the Celtic Tiger, there prevailed a common-place expression, " I wouldn't get out of bed for less than............", at which point some figure or condition was declared, indicating the speaker's sense of his own personal value.

And that's fair enough, we're all entitled to our views, and to any inoffensive means in expressing them.

However, depending on the company to whom it was expressed, the need to impress, or the amount of drink taken, figures and conditions tended to vary from reasonable to outrageous, often reflected, as the repetition began to take on the mantle of truth, like the current fake news, and assume an undeserved place in the annals of daily commerce.

But it was an interesting figure of speech.

What DOES get us out of bed in the morning?

What feeds the need to succeed? Money? To have it, or be seen to have it? Or a need for financial security?

Recognition? I've never met anyone who doesn't like some level of admiration, respect, deference, peer approval.

Accomplishment? To have accomplished anything in life is satisfying.

Power? Position, money, fame, can put the element of force in someone's grasp.

Freedom? The notion of Financial Freedom is an attraction for many of us. No more worries, no more sleepless nights about the wage bill, the rent, the taxman. The freedom of choice about the things we'd like for those we love, and for ourselves, without having to count it out and make it work with restrictive budgets.

Powerful motivators, all of them.

I imagine that most of us are touched by at least a couple, and maybe all, with emphasis on different ones.

Which brings us to the next question, and related to the question of last week; what gets you going?

What drives you?

And ask yourself, are you really driven by it, or is it just some kind of nice thing to think about, and if it comes, fine, and if it doesn't come, that's fine too.

And that really is fine too. Not everyone has to be driven to near distraction to achieve some goal. Some of us are ambitious. Some of us aren't.

Or we may be ambitious in that we like a quiet, undisturbed, orderly life, free of the urgency, the compulsion, the relentlessness, of *driving* ambition.

And that's fine too. We all have our roles to play, our responsibilities to fulfil, to ourselves and to others.

So, have a look at the question again. What drives you? It may be the desire for peace, quiet, solitude, or the need to succeed, to achieve, to climb the mountains, swim the rivers, blaze the trails.

Spend time. Have a good look at it. The answer you find is yours, and so long as it doesn't harm or encroach on another, it's your affair.

But do look. Explore. Discover. You can honour your ideas. You can be true to yourself.

The Science and Art of Mindset...

Many years ago, a man said to me, 'Whatever you're going to do, take the time to write it down, see it in your mind, and try to get the words on paper reflect the image in your mind'.

He was telling me to paint a word picture of whatever aim or aspiration I had. It still holds good for today. The likes of Harvard University, UCLA, and the University of British Columbia, have all established research indicating how the brain responds to precise direction and our emotions.

And that's a good reason to refresh our lives in the image of our goals, aims, aspirations.

When we think again about our potential, what we could achieve if we wanted to, if we were prepared to pay the price, if we set ourselves the task, and then decided and committed to it, our lives can take off again.

Speaking to a very successful writer recently, I was pleasantly surprised to hear that he starts every day, yes, every single day, with his Yoga moves, deep and active breathing exercises, and his mantra for the past four years, 'When I pursue my dream, my life is awake, and everything has meaning.'

He got the mantra from a quote by Charles Dickens. Now, there's a role model for anyone aspiring to write.

He won't start a day without that ritual.

Twenty years ago, that would have been thought 'too American', 'pie in the sky stuff', 'ok for the bird-brains, the dreamers.'

And that could be a fair point, *until you put into action what you've stated*, which changes everything.

As the University research strongly suggests, that's what gives meaning and direction to brain activity.

It's also called motivation, focus, active attention

A Mindful Exercise...

Lots of response to the last mail, nearly all of it pleasant and interesting.

So, to those of you who might be interested, here's an exercise to engage the mind, open the possibilities in life, and get the juices of creativity flowing into your days.

Get yourself a piece of paper, ten or fifteen minutes where you won't be disturbed, and a quiet spot.

Write this question on the paper, *'What do you believe, really believe, to be YOUR sense of purpose?'*

Give it the time it merits. Think of the question in terms of what's important to you currently in your life.

That might be your business, a relationship, a goal you've thought about for years, or even the desire to do less, quieten your life and hear the birds, look at the sky, and just be.

It's your choice, your privilege, and your affair.

Ask yourself earnestly. And answer truthfully.

Write this to yourself. No one else. It's no one else's business.

Go back to it, day after day. Let your mind become aware, steeped in the search for the answer to the question.

All kinds of possibilities begin to emerge, some surprisingly good ones, some outrageous.

And that's fine. It's a mental exercise, an exploration, not some exam to which you must apply the right formula.

There's no right, no wrong.

There's just you and your imagination, and your willingness to give it rein, let it rip, let the boundaries open as you begin to explore and visualize the potential of what's available to you and your life.

And you don't have to follow it. You can decide to do that. Or not.

Or you could decide that that's what you're capable of, so now you'll use half of your potential and just make a few small, comfortable changes, that just need a bit of attention and discipline, and consolidate and improve your life in a way you can handle.

Or you might decide to disrupt your life, make massive changes that turn your life inside out and bring you somewhere you never thought you'd reach...

Get yourself a little notebook. Write odd observations as they occur to you.

Keep your mind engaged with it. You'll become mindfully aware of your life, your own relationship with yourself, and you may get, as most do, a few useful and interesting insights to yourself and your life.

This is the kind of awareness that changes your self-talk, what you say to yourself about you, and your life.

Heed it well.

Fit for Purpose...?

Being well is a great privilege. It's not an entitlement. We must earn it, never more so than today, when despite our better standards of living, we can experience a lesser quality of life.

Ironic, isn't it?

Wellness comes from within. That's where the greatest gym' on the planet resides, underneath our skin.

When we use those resources, abilities, forces, available to us as part of our natural healing processes, we generally get for ourselves a state of wellness.

We'll also be more fit, and not just on a physical level, where we can run or climb or swim or jump, but more significantly, where we can be Fit for Purpose; for living, making the most of our own lives and those around us.

That's why we need to consider why we're doing a programme, a lifelong undertaking to keep ourselves healthy and well, and not just fit.

There's a difference.

Many people think being well is doing so many press-ups, bench presses, situps, or any other exercises, or that it's a case of not being sick.

But there's more to being well than just not being sick.

You can be up and about, doing your job, dealing with life, and not be well.

If you're tired, out of sorts, a bit run down, out of shape, just getting through a day is hard going.

And everything you face can be daunting.

It can be tough going, debilitating, overwhelming, a daily drudge.

Or it can be living.

If you're well, healthy, reasonably optimistic, energetic, you'll do things, you'll try things, and you'll achieve things that otherwise wouldn't even be on the radar.

Science is now proving what we've all believed all along; a healthy body promotes a healthy mind, and a healthy mind develops a healthy body

The Power of Mindful Awareness...

Small changes, little switches here and there, brief interludes regularly practiced, all contribute to a mighty change.

If change is what you want.

But you don't have to turn your world upside down, alienate your family and friends, create enmity in your life.

No. Mindful Awareness is a mental exercise, a useful way of disciplining your mind, and your habits.

That's the way it works.

If you let it.

It pervades daily life, improving posture, breathing patterns, habits, which have a positive effect on the mind, focusing on positive activity, in search of a positive outcome, creating a positive state of expectancy.

It can trim you down, tone you up, and resurrect energy you never knew you had.

Alphabet of Health... (O W N)...again

Create a solid foundation for good health with the following, Oxygen, Water and Nutrition.

The first requirement of every cell in your body is for oxygen. How you breathe, ventilate your system, enliven your body cells, has a huge influence on your health.

That's why there's such an emphasis on exercising, it makes you breathe more fully, opening the lungs, oxygenating the blood and saturating your system in the force of life that oxygen brings.

If you don't have the time or the desire to exercise, teach yourself to breathe, regularly, deeply, steadily.

You'll be more relaxed, energized and healthy.

Secondly, you need water. We're meant to be about 60-65% water. That's the amount of fluid we need in the body for the chemistry to take place. If you're dehydrated, it can't happen. The system doesn't work, and you get tired, irritable, constipated, out of sorts, liable to all kinds of colds, fatigue, ailments.

Get about two litres of water a day into your system.

Nutrition, as opposed to just putting what is often disguised as food into ourselves these days, is vital.

You can do this simply. Get whole foods. Anything that walks, swims, flies or grows, you can eat. That's whole food, from the earth, with vitamins, minerals, trace elements, protein, and a small amount of natural sugar and starch and fats, all of which, when taken in reasonable balance, will help the growth, maintenance and repair of your cells. And keep you healthy.

I'd recommend a good multivitamin/mineral tablet every morning too. It won't do you any harm and may do you the world of good, compensating for the processes our poor food endures on its way to our plates.

There's a start for the summer, now racing in on us.

Do this for a start. Stick with it. Get the habit. Be well.

Decisions, decisions, decisions.

Every single moment of any day, we're deciding a direction, one way or another.

And the power in giving direction to our lives is in the small, daily, hourly, minute-by-minute decisions which we can tend to dismiss as insignificant.

But they're the ones that count. They're the ones that create a trend, form a habit, give a direction to our lives.

Making decisions that move us in a direction, however minute, create pathways in our lives, and in our minds.

Physical habits, and mental habits, form lifestyle actions and neural pathways, in our existence, so subtle, that we don't even see them happening.

Which is why that the beginning of a habit can be so unobtrusive, we don't even feel it, but by the time it's formed, it's so strong we can't even contemplate breaking it.

And that's one of the reasons why making a huge change in your life, often best and most effectively begins with a small change here, *a subtle change there, and the simple wit and persistence to stay on it.*

In other words, by becoming constantly mindful, and quietly aware, of how you're thinking, you can, with the same powerful means that once bound you to a habit, now use that very same means to change the pattern, redirect your energies, and take you where you want to go.

And simple it is. Not always easy, but simple. And doable, as anyone who's done it will tell you.

Decision for YOU...

Had some interesting comments on the last mail, the one about decisions.

Here's what came out of it; the people who wrote told me that they'd started to do something in a very small way, like learning a guitar, or painting, or getting a bit more fit, or being a bit more tolerant, or learning how to breathe.

What they said was that they'd started to do something, however small, every day. This was key to every letter I got. And it really pointed up the value of constancy. If you do something, every day, you create an awareness of it. And that's the key; awareness.

That's what nags your conscience, plays at the back of your mind, won't let go. It's called habit.

And habits are as hard to break, as they're easy to form.

So, let's get back to taking a decision. Decide on something NOW. Some little or big thing you've been threatening to do for ages but haven't got around to doing.

Then ACT on it. Do something about it, even if it's only to write a note to yourself to do it again tomorrow. And do that every day, some small step you can deal with, put into action and continue.

All results are cumulative. The more frequently they're done, the more they form a pattern of activity, the more entrenched they become in your mind and in your life.

They work the same way compound interest does on money. All the accumulated experience is added to the new experience and reinforces the pattern and the result.

So, whether you want to write a book, make a million, be a good human being, start now. With a bit of persistence, a bit of will, and a sound belief in the worth of your aims, you'll get there. Maybe sooner, maybe later.

But you'll be a hell of a longer way than you were at the starting point, wherever it takes you.

And simple it is. Not always easy, but simple. And doable, as anyone who's done it will tell you.

As my dear friend and mentor, Jake, back in the nineteen fifties, told me;

'Take a decision, do it with a will, see it through.'

I didn't appreciate what he was telling me at the time. What Jake was saying was that you need to start with something you believe you can do, and genuinely want to have done. *Then start. Get at it. Finish it off.*

Do some simple thing you know you can achieve, but have been putting off, perhaps for no better reason that you just didn't want to do it.

But you want it done.

So now, take your decision, do it with a will, and see it through.

Friday, bedamned.... TGIM

Attitude is vital in any undertaking.

It's the effect on the surface of the underlying currents; physical well-being, mental stability, emotional force, personal spirit, energy.

One current expression in today's language can betray an attitude that isn't always helpful. It's 'Thank God It's Friday'.

Which is ok. Friday can be a welcome respite from a battling week, but it comes with a condition; provided we apply the same value to poor old Monday. Monday has traditionally been a day of penitence. We tend to think of it as a day to be resigned to, to endure.

Better experience of life could be felt by making Monday a highlight day too, greeting it with enthusiasm, energy, anticipation. Don't you think so?

'TGIM' is a worthy aim for anyone wanting to achieve an aim, score a goal in life's game, or who harbours any aspiration.

Monday is a good day.

It's a restart, a fresh look, another chance. And as the first day of the rest of the week, it's an ideal day to start a project.

And Friday is a good day to plan the following Monday. You can organise your action, and yourself, and then enjoy a diverting weekend clear in the knowledge that you'll hit the ground running on Monday.

Which gives the week a great start. So, try this. Many have, with truly startling results.

Go to your diary NOW. Go to the diary on Friday. and put in a reminder to plan your following Monday. THEN ACT ON YOUR PLAN.

Do that for the following 8 weeks.

Then watch your weeks take an effect, a direction, a momentum, that will give those weeks, and your life, and your TGIM, a resounding and scintillating reality.

Hurling Up a Storm in Business...

The magnificent Henry Sheflin, Kilkenny Icon, Other Counties' Nemesis, recently did a documentary on how the mind behaves in the process of winning.

Now Henry wasn't just talking about winning a hurling match, or walloping in another goal for the Black and Amber, he was talking about *how the mind contributes to the notion, and the act, of winning,* and how this knowledge can be transferred to any endeavour.

He had suitably qualified professors to back up what he said, and even had them demonstrate how it affects us as humans. We can set our minds, and most significantly, our emotions, and programme ourselves accordingly, to behave in a way that supports our goals in life.

This was seen in a few instances, one being where Roger Bannister broke the so-called unbreakable four-minute-mile in 1954, and how thirty eight people, some of them Bannister's detractors and critics, did the very same over the next twelve months.

This was an example of how the power of belief changed the physical performance.

One day, the belief wasn't there, the next day, it was. And that belief allowed the runner to find the resources within himself to reach the goal, break the barrier.

And that was the theme of the whole programme, the mental barrier; how belief can limit, and how it can liberate.

Dr. Shane O'Mara of TCD called it the difference between the FIXED mind and the GROWTH mind.

We've all seen this in play at some time or other in our lives.

We find ourselves in a crisis, think the world's falling around us, and then, after some time, find a way of dealing with the worst of the situation.

Then we find something else that even lessens the impact on our lives. And then we find another viewpoint that opens possibilities we'd never have considered before, We then see how to turn the whole event into an advantage, an asset, something we can use to enhance our lives.

What's happened is within us, not in outside circumstances.

The circumstances are the same, but we've changed our viewpoint, taken a different approach, and turned it, and our experience of it, into a discovery, often revealing attributes we had forgotten, or didn't even know, we had.

And it goes for anything in life. But there is one condition that must be fulfilled; you need to DO something about it.

You can know all about how to do something, what needs to be done, but nothing happens *till you move on it.*

And that came across strongly in a clip in which Enda McNulty worked on the visualisation techniques with a lead dancer in Riverdance.

The dancer learned the method, then practised and practised it. And guess what. He got good at it, and the thought processes carried over to his anticipation for the stage entry, and then into the performance itself.

What the programme showed was that the same method can be used in any avenue in life, any avenue at all.

And that's what Mindful Awareness is about; being aware of how you're using that wonderful piece of Biological Magic that is available to us all.

Do well and have a healthy and creative day.

Mindful Awareness and Nonsense...

Mindful awareness is a useful skill. Scientific research is showing how it can clear the mind, soothe the nerves, bring a sense of calm and quiet purpose to life.

Even more recent research shows how it can be used to change how you use your brain, improve learning, and redirect the mental habits of a lifetime.

But like a lot of esoteric skills, it can be used to confuse, confound, create doubt and instability.

It's not a magic wand. It depends on how you learn it.

There is nothing, absolutely nothing, false about the real moment-to-moment awareness, a state of mind where your awareness of the world you're in, and your presence in it, inform your thoughts and emotions, so that you can make the most of who you can be when you're at your best.

It's no coincidence either that Mindful Awareness, and many other of the Mind / Body disciplines, use our basic functions and senses, like breathing, standing, balance, listening, looking, for their practice.

People who do these, with a bit of will and devotion, have found a whole new perception of health, wellness, fitness, and the means to enjoying them.

Their sense of awareness, brought about by intelligent practice, becomes a force in their lives, allowing them to adapt to the changes that they need for whatever aims they choose to pursue.

Physical and mental health improve, often beyond expectation. Energy levels rise, attention span expands, bringing a new and vibrant quality to life.

And it is as simple as that; not often easy, but simple.

You just need to know *what* to do; know *how* to do it; and then *get on with it.*

Three Things Healthy People Do...

There are people who hate the thought of training. They regard the Fitness Culture, the Gym Culture, the ballyhoo that surrounds the Nutrition Industry, with disdain.

And they have a point. There has always been an elitist element in the fitness scene, much of it centred round a rampant narcissism that repels as much as it attracts.

That's why the definition, and the purpose, of being fit, needs to be clear.

I can only speak for myself here and say what it means to me. Maybe this may strike a chord with you, or maybe it won't.

In youth, I enjoyed a fairly good level of athletic ability, and enthusiasm, and saw the benefits in other areas of my life. Apart from the necessity to be fit for sport, it also became, in my view, a necessity for living a useful and enjoyable, life.

It helped me feel well, concentrate ably, maintain energy, and support an attitude necessary for what I needed to do. They're the benefits of being fundamentally well.

And that belief, reinforced over the years, is amply supported by empirical and scientific evidence today.

So for our purpose, I'm defining fitness as a means to an end; the end being healthy, productive and enjoyable living, for *whatever* your aims are.

I've also seen that people who are basically fit, feeling well, and optimizing on their personal resources and abilities, have at least three things in common.

Firstly, they know how, and take the trouble, to ventilate their systems. They tend to do this either on purpose or instinctively. They're active enough, or breathe in a certain way, to make sure their lungs work well.

This brings the force of life to the cellular level, bringing energy, vitality, vigour, to every cell in the body.

Secondly, they hydrate adequately. They get enough fluid in their systems to allow the body chemistry take place.

Thirdly, they are aware of what, and how, they eat.

Without being monastic, they put into their systems what helps maintain, repair and positively affect the function of their body cells. And that's what nutrition comes down to; eating to live, as opposed to living to eat.

No deep mystery. No complication. Keep it simple. And persist.

Start there.

Full Marks to The Irish Times...

One of the best articles written about training, fitness, and being healthy and well, appeared recently in the Irish Times.

It spoke of over-training, doing too much too often, and the consequent disastrous effects.

It's about time something like it appeared in a daily journal.

The trend in gyms, magazines, TV programmes tends to amplify the notion that more is better, harder is essential, and that unless you're in the six-pack, barn-door back, muscle-slabbed, coconut-shoulder brigade, you're a dilettante, amateur, even wasting your time.

Which was exactly the philosophy that destroyed the aspirations of many sensible, hopeful, conscientious people who wanted to learn how to get fit, healthy and well.

There is more to being well than just being fit.

Fitness may let you sprint for the bus, run a marathon, even do a triathlon, but if it's not geared to your well-being, your personal ideals, and to what your happiness criterion may be for life, it can be as damaging as it can be beneficial.

Being Well and Healthy, however, is something else.

When you're in a state of balance, when your body and your mind are in tune, when your emotions are stable, you experience life on a different level.

Of course, you'll have emotional, mental, and physical, ups and downs. C'est la vie.

But in general, training your mind, practising the habit of awareness, and by applying simple principles of body toning and conditioning, you'll create an overall shape, and a feel to your life, that you'll find much more supportive, and readily accessible.

More significantly, you'll find it sustainable. And as it self-perpetuates, it improves naturally.

This is no deep mystery. As most people using this kind of system observe, there's a lot of plain common sense to it.

Being well and healthy may not be the panacea to life's travails, but it sure helps cope with them.

It's well worth remembering that what often overwhelms us in life, is not so much the challenge we face, as how we respond to it.

How Me, Tony Doran And The Wexford Hurling Team, Won The 1968 All-Ireland Hurling Final...

Here's a memory that All-Ireland Hurling weekend never fails to evoke...

The afternoon stretched out before me.

It was 1968. We'd just finished a Sunday lunch gig in the "Green Man" pub, Blackheath Common, South London. The instruments had been loaded into the van. Our work was done for the day.

I said my goodbyes to the boys of the band. There are times when the only way to be is solitary. A vague anxiety hovered somewhere in the back of my mind. I couldn't fix a name to it, or a cause. It wasn't even that there was anything wrong.

It just didn't feel right.

I felt without direction, unsettled, aimless.

And that was how my mind responded; aimlessly.

Moving from the Common, I found myself wandering into Lewisham High Street.

In those days most shops were shut on Sundays. The street was a canyon of glass and concrete, with people meandering, strolling, up and down, window-shopping, chatting, looking, buying tea at the tea stalls, all moving slowly in the warm September sun.

Behind a tea stall at which I had stopped, was a barrow full of books, all hardbacks, with their spines turned up. Picking up what turned out to be an old English reader, with essays by the likes of Hazlitt, Charles Lamb, Dickens, a page dropped open on "The Wayfarer", the poem by Pádraic Pearse.

There, amid the roar of traffic, the walls of hot sun-reflecting glass, the chug of buses and the crowd on the sun-brightened city concrete, my eye fell on the words,

"… To see a leaping squirrel in a tree,

Or a red ladybird upon a stalk,

Or little rabbits in a field at evening,

Lit by a slanting sun, on some green hill,

Where shadows drifted by…"

And they took my breath away.

I paid the 6p for the tea, three pennies for the book, and moved on. Turning down an alleyway which wound down to the green square in Catford where I lived, I was now surrounded by tall chestnuts and beeches, with the sun dappling through the leaves and branches in shadowed patterns on the short, manicured grass of the square.

I was heading for a wooden bench in the sunny gap between two trees when I was brought to a standstill by a strident high and familiar voice.

From an open window on the far side of the green, Miceál O'Héihir was sounding the halftime score of the All Ireland Hurling Final.

Like filings to a magnet, I was drawn across the green. "And the Wexford men are traipsing off" intoned Miceál.

A face appeared in the open window. "Where are you from?" Asked the face.

"Wexford" I answered.

"A Jaysus! We're batin' the shite out o' yiz", he exclaimed. "Come on in! Hear in the second half!"

"Thanks", I said "leave the window open, I'll sit here on the wall."

On the wall, with my back to the window, I sat looking over the small green. But I wasn't seeing that green patch of grass in a square in South East London.

I was seeing the green fields and the rolling hills of south county Wexford, the back roads and the winding lanes, the high hedges and the looping Hawthorne. I was hearing the rattle of the empty billycan on the handlebars of the bike on the old dusty road, the chirrup of birds in the hedgerow, that early evening birdsong, the bark of a dog as I passed a gate, the greeting, ‹grand day› from a passing farmer, as I made my way to Grant's farm to to collect the milk for the following day.

But then a Croke Park roar interrupted my reverie.

The second-half was starting. Miceál was announcing the throw -in. The cheering and the roaring filled the air.

"Wexford are eight points down!... A wide for Tipperary!", Shouted Miceál "...pucks it out... Phil Wilson catches....bursts past Babs Keating...runs through Jimmy Doyle. ...flicks it over to Jack Berry! Here come the Boys of Wexford!" Roared Miceál, his voice rising, excitement mounting...

."a pass back to Paul Lynch...Paul looks up, steadies and strikes...and it's over the bar! A point for Wexford!!

This looks like a different Wexford team from the first half...". The rest of his words were lost in the voice of the entire Wexford county as it roared the team on.

"...a long puck out...a bobbing ball...Dan Quigley gathers."

Some of his words were getting lost in bursting roars from the crowd in Croke Park.

Amid the background din came names and words that meant that the Wexford men were fighting back. The name Dan Quigley came up again,… "What a catch! Flips it over to Ned Colfer!

Colfer to Willie Murphy!

Murphy to Phil Wilson!

Phil turns and fires it up the field! It's coming down!.

Tony Doran is in there!! So is Christy Jacob! So is Seamus Whelan!

"Up goes Tony! He catches! Holds, and swivels.!

He palms the ball!

He shortens the grip and with a mighty twist of the shoulders *buries* it in the Tipperary net!"

"The game has changed!, "shouted Miceál into the microphone and out to the world. "The Boys of Wexford are hurling back! This is a different team! It's a different game from the first half!"

A roar drowned his commentary as Wexford pumped another one over the bar.

The noise from the crowd and the speed of commentary melded into a continuous stream of sound as the Wexford men hurled their way into the game…"Wexford 2 goals and six points, Tipperary, one goal and twelve points!" shouted Miceál. "Only three points in it! Who'd have thought it at half time!?!

Wexford had been trailing by 8 points. They looked beaten, bedraggled, done! It must be the spirit of 1798," continued Miceál,

"….the Boys of Wexford! Fighting with heart and hand!"

The game roared on.

Down the field it came. Wexford were hurling like men possessed. Purple and gold were bursting up the field again. Down came the ball.

Up went the hands!

The roar of the crowd filled the square in Catford.

The two teams hurled it out in Croke Park.

And I was hurling it out in Catford, Southeast London!

Off the wall, seeing the green of Croke park in my mind's eye, the jerseys of the Blue and Gold of Tipperary, and my own

Purple and Gold of the Model County, my heart and mind and spirit were hurling air, swinging arms, screaming and shouting as I heard it on the radio and saw the spectacle in my head.

'...another one for Wexford' shouted Miceál. Tipperary one goal and twelve points, Wexford three goals and six points.....the teams are level!!"

Hysteria throttled up my throat and roared the Wexford men on! Out come Tony Doran again! The square was a frenzied maelstrom of Blues and Purple and the flashes of Purple and Gold as hands and heads and scything hurls flashed in the air. Then a mighty roar lifted Jimmy O'Brien's Hurley and smite it against the tiny white sphere once more to the Tipperary net !!!

Wexford four goals and six points! Tipperary one goal and twelve points.

On they hurled! The men in Croke Park, battling every ball, hunting every chance, hooking, blocking, tackling through the game!

And there was I, in Catford, swinging, dodging, palming, so that when Jack Berry belted in Goal number five, London, in the United Kingdom, just like Tipperary, in the Republic of Ireland, was at the mercy of anything Wexford.

To seal the game, our Tony pumped over another point, just before a desperate but willing Tipperary punched the Wexford net with their second goal of the game.

On we hurled, Tony and the boys in Croke Park, Me in South London. We hurled and we tackled and we blocked and we hooked and we pointed and we ran and we played till our legs and our lungs and our shoulders screamed for relief.

The pitch was getting bigger and the ball was getting smaller, the lifting of the stick was like hauling it through thick mud.

Heart and Soul, I was there with them on that green patch of grass across the breadth of England and over the Irish Sea, hauling aching limbs and indomitable minds through those last few minutes of physical hell.

And then it went; that shrill, thin, lung-long blast of the game-end whistle.

And we, Tony and the boys in Croke Park, and me, in a distant corner of South East London, and the men and the women and the boys and the girls of the county of Wexford, had won!

We had won the All Ireland Hurling Final!

Sitting on that wall , back to the window, a kaleidoscope of visions and sights running through the hungry eyes of my turbulent mind, the relief, the elation, the welling pride, the rediscovery, the sense of place, of identity, the exquisite sadness, erupted through my system in mighty body-shocking sobs.

"What're ye bawlin' about?", demanded Tipperary. He was leaning on the wall a foot or two away from me. He held a packet of Gold Flake in one hand, a lighter in the other. 'Have a fag', he offered, 'it'll hold ye together.'

"Yah", he continued" It's hard to be here when that's goin' on over there. It'll be a lonely day for many a one of yere county."

To the background of speeches, declarations for Wexford, commiserations for Tipp', coming from the radio, I moved from the wall, feeling my feet plant firmly and decisively on the concrete of the pathway. Turning to that kindly Tipperary Man, I heard my own voice utter the words "I'm going home."

It was a simply stated declaration.

And it wasn't talking about the small apartment around the corner; in Catford, South East London, which I had casually called my home, the place where I currently lay my head, where I slept, where I ate.

No.

It was to green fields and the high ditches, winding lane ways and hidden farmhouses, birds in a clear sky, warm quiet greetings on the roads, chance meetings at crossroads, rabbits in the fields at evenings, lit by slanting suns on green hills, where shadows drifted by.....

That was the home to which I was going.

And subsequently went.

The Truth About Mindfulness...

The understanding of Mindfulness can be confusing.

It's been said that in the last ten years, more has been discovered about brain function than in the previous ten decades.

Discovery has designated the brain as the New Frontier in humanity.

Science is now confirming what most of have believed all along; that everything comes from the mind, and that we can learn how to use the mind as we use any instrument.

Previously, it was thought that a person's character, attitude, mindset, were formed indelibly by about the age of seven or so.

Recent research has indicated that by understanding Neuroplasticity, the variable qualities of the human brain, we can alter our core beliefs, change our attitudes, and command a mindset of our choice.

Changes in lives, experiences, and perceptions are taking place, at all ages.

This opens all kinds of possibilities to anyone who cares to use it.

Even more recent research at the University of British Colombia suggests that we can use different strategies to affect this phenomenon.

It's been seen that there are three ways in which we can do this; chemically, physically, and functionally.

Chemical changes take place as you use your brain, neurons affecting each other by transference.

You positively affect your brain by exercise, as we in the Western world know it, but even more so by practising the Yoga, Tai Chai, activities that generate vital energy.

We affect the brain by directing energies, setting goals, recognising aspirations, and then driving our efforts in that direction.

Being mindfully aware of this, and putting it to practical use, can help you decide what course to take to support your aspirations, whatever they may be.

And that's what Mindful Awareness is about. It's a mental skill, and like all skills, has its fundamentals, and they can be learned.

Age Can Change Your Lung Capacity...

It's an established fact that between the ages of 35 and 60, lung capacity in the average man or woman can diminish by up to 50%.

This is not due to illness or injury, but from disuse.

Yes, disuse.

This then leads to shallow breathing, muscle tension, poor circulation, lack of oxygen to the brain cells, fatigue, lowered resistance to colds, flu', sickness, which in turn affects energy, misaligns posture, aggravates the already worsening condition, brings on debilitation, sickness and even early death.

All from disuse.

Get your thinking cap on; breathe well, and have that magnificent piece of physical equipment, your pulmonary system, working for you, and not against you.

Harmony in Life...

Breathing power is not just about the ability to get oxygen into our blood, but about the ability too, to create the phenomenon known as *entrainment*, commonly called *harmony*, in our lives.

When our systems work in harmony, we are at ease; the opposite to being ill at ease, and then DIS-eased.

At ease, our physical, mental, spiritual, emotional systems exist in harmony.

They help each other perform.

They perform more easily, fluently, naturally.

Be at ease.

Breathe.

Muhammed Ali on Golf...

"Float like a butterfly, sting like a bee", went the simple but effective philosophy of Muhammed Ali, the boxer who could fight, the fighter who could box.

I knew people who adopted the slogan to their own lives; it made sense. It described the ability to travel in cruise control, with the ability to kick the pedal, floor it, and accelerate with blinding speed when needed.

It's a great quality. DJ Carey was, and I'm sure still is, a master. You could see him prowling about the pitch, reading the game, feeling the tempo, moving with the ebb and flow of activity.

Then, responding to instinct, you'd see him position himself, receive the ball, assume the goal-bound crouch, and accelerating with devastating pace, dazzle the crowd, blind his opponents, and deliver a murderous shot to the to a pin-point target in the net.

Performers of this calibre have a common denominator; no doubt.

There isn't a hint of doubt in a pitch's distance about their ability.

So, when someone told me about an interview in which Ali called himself the Greatest Golfer in the World, I wasn't surprized at what he'd said. But I was surprised that he played golf. I'd never heard of him being a golfer, or read of him playing that game.

Neither had anyone else whom I asked.

Then my late, wonderful friend and mentor, who had also heard the interview, explained the context.

The interviewer had asked what else he was good at, and Ali had answered that whatever he might decide to do, he would bend every moment, every muscle, fibre, breath and effort in his existence to be the very best he could be, at it.

So, he said he would be the best in the world, at whatever it was he decided to do. Hence, he described himself as the Greatest Golfer in The World; he just hadn't got around to doing it yet.

To be prepared to do what is necessary to achieve an aim in life, is to display the ability to train, learn, practise, research, rehearse and discipline the mind, heart, soul, and actions to that end; to pay the price.

Most of us don't necessarily want to be the best in the world, but we do have aims, ideals, aspirations, that can bring a vitality, energy and real meaning to our lives.

When we acknowledge them. And they too, do need practice, drill, rehearsal, to get done.

They also need our recognition, and the courage of our decision to pursue them.

That's why we need to be able to stop every now and again, consider what aims we have, or think we have, and seriously consider what we're DOING about them.

It doesn't matter what the aim is; it's your aim and it's your business. But it matters mightily that we search for it, consider it, and then decide to do it. Or leave it.

When we decide to pursue an aim, the world comes alive and everything, everything, has meaning.

Good man, Ali.

A Bit About the Secret...

When you eat regularly and well, you get your blood sugar levels in place.

Now that's key.

You'll have energy. Lots of it. And you won't have to deal with those cravings for sugary snacks.

You'll have great metabolism, body fat loss, improved muscle tone. Your ability to think, and to concentrate for long periods, benefit enormously. Get your food choices in first, then your exercises and routines. Everything happens naturally after that.

Remember you O W N your condition. That's about getting **O**xygen, **W**ater and **N**ourishment into your system.

That simply means that when you breathe well, get adequate water, about one and a half to two litres a day, and take the trouble to get the appropriate foods into your body, you get well, healthy and fit.

Being well and healthy is about being aware of the basic laws of nature

Allow for them, use them, keep the practice simple, and it's impossible for your body not to respond.

Too much of anything brings about imbalance.

There's the key word for you; balance. It's a natural inclination when you give yourself the chance to experience it.

But first you must think about it, openly. Let yourself listen to what sometimes sounds like rubbish when you hear it first. Then evaluate in your own time, digest the knowledge you gain, and when you've done that, you can assimilate it and come to your own conclusions.

Start with a food diary.

Do it for 21 days. Be meticulous. Record everything. Regard it as an exercise in observation. That's your first discipline.

Start there.

Tired? Fatigued? Running Low on Juice?...

Do this; on the night before your next day, decide what you want to think about in the first 10 minutes of the following morning, what you want to focus on, be aware of, have in your mind for the day.

Then follow through. Just do that.

Then do it for the next 21 nights and days.

Without fail.

As soon as you start, your life awakens in the true sense, in those mornings.

But only do it if you want to.

This simple practice has turned peoples' lives around.

Health Warning...

According to research by the Economic Social Research Institute in conjunction with The World Health Organisation, Ireland will be, by 2030, the fattest, most overweight, unfit country in the European Community.

When you think that we were once famed as scholars, producing GIANTS in the literary, arts, business and entertainment worlds, sending out a genius from West Cork in the early part of the last century, when he accelerated the fledgling motor industry, and put Ford cars on the road, changing the way of transport on the planet for ever, when one of the greatest Presidents of the U.S.A, and a World Leader, descended from emigrants from the hinterlands of my own County Wexford, we seem to have lost our way somewhere.

We're now in danger of becoming that tiny geographical couch on the shelf of the European Continent, where rotting potatoes, flaccid marshmallows, and television sponges languish.

Not an exciting prospect.

Where to start? Schools? Politicians? Businesses? Associations? Churches?

Or how about the homes?

If the population of any land is thought to be the sum of the individuals in it, it 'd seem sensible for each unit to look after its own, wouldn't it? Then each home would take care of the nutritional value of the food eaten in the house, the quality of nourishment each occupant experiences, and make a strong contribution to the level of health enjoyed by each occupant.

But that's only my idea.

Maybe we should we ignore it and hope it'll go away? Or pretend it doesn't even exist? Or is it something that can be managed? Or changed? Or influenced?

I believe it can be influenced.

Any suggestions?

Heart Attack...!!!

Looking back over a piece written by Dr. Al Sears, it was reported that 50% of all heart attacks are caused by lack of oxygen reserves.

This makes sense when you think that lung capacity from the age of about 35 begins to diminish in most people. The reduction comes not from illness or injury.

It comes from disuse.

'Use it or lose it' really is applicable here, isn't it?

So, whether you're into exercise, training, gym work or whatever, get into your breathing practice.

You don't have to huff, puff, get obsessive about it. Just practice breathing on a regular basis.

It helps calm the mind

It relaxes muscles and reduces unnecessary tension.

It opens blood vessels.

It take pressure off heart and arteries.

It ventilates the system in a way that no other exercise can.

When you breathe deeply and with attention, from the diaphragm, you actively train the muscles involved in the process, which then, thus trained, come into play when you're under exertion, or tense, or in a potentially stressful time.

It's a simple enough action. It's significant too, that those who've taken this to heart enjoy more energy, sharper focus, and much greater resistance to illness, fatigue, distress.

Now, remember the three principles in the successful outcome of any endeavour;

Know what to do.

Know how to do it.

Get on with it.

Lobster Pots and Life Lessons

Bill, a life-long fisherman in his late 60's, and who could read the weather instinctively, was leaning on the railing of the pier, looking down into our boat 'Wind's getting' up. There's a chop on the water,' he continued. 'Anyone'd have a hard time out in that. Time for prudence'

The words were said as articles of faith, beyond advice, more than wisdom. They were uttered as canons of direction, spoken in a tone of finality, not to be questioned, no hint of doubt. That was the way it was.

But they were said to a man who respected his own counsel. Jake had his own mind. He knew the power of the wind, the run of the waves, how his 26' clinker-built converted lifeboat,

'Hesperian', could work the sea, could shift her way windward, could roll and dive in the waves.

So he went out.

There were seven lobster pots for hauling, slightly south of the Forlorn Headland, a short sail out and as far as Jake was concerned, could be done in quick time and be back before the storm hit. He looked at me, 'Ready?'

'Sure am', I replied. I'd have gone in any weather with Jake.

The wind was rising. An ebbing tide-run threw a steep chop in the waves.

We rigged 'Hesperian', set the sails, and casting off quickly from the slipway, ghosted across the calm of the harbour till we came to the mouth and the opening out into the sea.

Once out from under the lee of the pier, the squall hit. Hesperian heeled, slanting the full set of sails and the tall mast across the clouds. Jake pointed her high into the wind and we ploughed forward, plumes of spray rising and drenching us as we crashed on in steady, pounding progress.

With the lee gunwale often awash, a hard wind gusting at times to a heavy force, we moved relentlessly on a starboard tack to the lobster ground.

After just under an hour, we were where we needed to be. Seated high on the weather gunwale, I scoured for, and sighted, the first of the buoys. These were attached to the lobster pots, deep beneath the angry seas. We'd gone a bit beyond them. We would have to go back, get downwind of them and then make the approach.

With the gusting wind, the fast-running seas, and the deeper troughs out where we were, going about and getting to the lee of the pots would be tricky. Jake told me to drop the topsail. I undid the cleated halyard, jerked once and hard. The triangular canvass at the masthead guttered and flapped and slid with a clatter at my feet. I gathered the wet canvass, folding it roughly and ramming it under the foredeck.

'Ready about', roared Jake.

'Say when', I shouted back, flipping the jib-sheets off the cleats and getting them ready to back them off and get us turned more quickly.

Hesperian, fully under way, ran into the wind, never paused, never faltered, but did a clean about-turn into a close-reach run to bring us down to the lee of the pots.

'Hold hard.', roared Jake. He let the main go, turning her into the wind. We rose and crashed in the shortening chop to where the first buoy in the line lifted and dipped in the running seas.

There were no words after that. We knew the drill.

Taking out the boathook, I leaned into the rolling water and dragged the buoy back in over the side. Gripping hard, hand over hand, I raised the reluctant pot and lifted it in.

Jake now had the jib sheets. He let one go, the flapping, rampant canvass adding to the racket the mainsail was already making.

Foot by foot, wave by trough, Jake held Hesperian on the pot-line, rising and dipping, just enough off the wind to keep her under way. He let her ride and hold through the driving walls of charging water.

The wind was rising.

I worked incessantly, lifting the buoys, hauling the ropes, raising the pots, wrestling them aboard, letting them fall where they may. By the fifth pot, my arms ached. My back was throbbing with fatigue. As I got that fifth pot to the surface and alongside the gunwale, a rogue wave rolled in under the hull, lifting the bow a couple of impossible feet. I was holding hard onto the pot. It was pulling me in, inch by rapid inch over the side. Jake released the jib, moved to the mid seat. Only for him catching me by the hair, pulling me back, and lifting me bodily back aboard, these words might not be getting written.

I landed on the floorboards, rope and pot and rolling buoy along with me. 'Take her' shouted Jake. 'I'll haul the other two'.

I took the tiller, found the jib-sheet, and held her on the line for the next two pots.

Jake hooked buoy number six, and in a strong hand-over-hand working of the rope, ripped the pot from the sea and threw it on the crowding floor.

One to go.

'Come on', he roared, 'let's get it'. I eased the wave-dancing Hesperian to the last and mocking buoy. I hauled the jib, worked the tiller, and eked up near the tossing buoy.

Jake leaned, hooked and grabbed the buoy, and as if asserting himself in the crashing, tumbling, elements about him, fought the pot aboard and flung it on the floorboards.

'Let's go', he shouted over the now roaring seas and the flap and crack of the sails. I gave him the tiller, moved to the forward seat, hauled on the jib-sheets.

He let her a couple of points off the wind, and the sails filled. The hull settled.

Then we were scooting over the running waves, diving with the rolling foam and rush of the sea, on a fast broad reach. We were almost on a dead straight run off the wind. The mainsail bellied, the jibs ballooned.

Hesperian ran, rolled, skipped and crashed her way as she'd never done before. We were surfing and sailing, lifting on a fast wave, catching the wind up high and diving into the fast running trough of water ahead. The centre-board was humming in a low rumble with the speed of the hull and the rush of the seas. We held course, gripping timber, working the sheets, shifting our weight, as Hesperian came alive and lifted and crashed her way in the rolling seas in that turbulent run for land and shelter.

We'd never come home as fast. After what seemed like minutes, we were approaching the harbour. The seas lessened as we ran to the back of the pier, the small headland giving a some shelter, making the difference between dangerous and hard.

Though gusting treacherously, the wind was less, the seas quieter, and Hesperian relaxed into an even momentum to the harbour mouth. We rounded the end of the pier, entering the shelter and protection of the anchorage in a calm and quiet sigh of relief. We dropped the main, one of the jibs. Hesperian whispered across the calm and welcoming surface of the harbour to the slipway.

I raised the centre-board, hooked it up, and went to the bow to catch the iron ladder on the wall.

Recovered and relieved, I stepped up the ladder and fastened the painter to the big iron bollard on the quay. Jake threw up the aft line and I made it fast to the other bollard.

A couple of men were strolling up to where we were. I went back aboard and helped Jake with the pots.

We piled the pots on the slipway. Looking at the catch, I could see Jake was pleased. Ten lobsters, all decent, one huge, a couple of crabs, and a very disturbed and angry Conger Eel.

The men on the pier had gathered above us. One of them, Bill, pulled a pipe from his mouth, saying, 'Got back just in time. Blowin' up hard now. More on the way.'

Not looking up, Jake answered quietly, 'Aye. It's all about the timin'.'

'Nice catch', Bill conceded, adding 'An' ye've a good crew.'

This time Jake did look up, and giving me a gentle thump on the shoulder, said, 'The best.'

In those days, twelve-year-olds, when in adult company, were allowed to listen to, but not be part of, the conversation.

I carried on, pretending to be unaffected by the compliment. As if I hadn't heard it.

But to this day, sixty-five years later, those simply stated words, on that wet and blustery day, on a windswept rainy pier, burn bright and incandescent in the warmth of memory.

Training the Mind...

There's a lot of talk about meditation these days. No harm either. Awareness is raised, and we become more conscious of it as a practical thing to do. And practical, it is.

For long, it's been associated with the Beard, Robe and Sandal Brigade. It was as if they had appropriated it into their style and made it exclusive. And that could have been the intention. We humans as a race sometimes can give an elitism to what we do, to make it look, or sound, more accomplished, and by reflection, elevate our own image. That's a part of being human.

Meditation, however, is a practice. Most people can do it. It takes a bit of discipline, rehearsal, patience, and determination.

Which is why it is eminently suitable to people who think they're not the 'meditative type'.

It means, for a result to take place, that the person who needs it most, can be taught, and then train themselves, how to do it. It's the same as learning how to exercise. We use our minds to learn exercise movements. Meditation is a form of exercise.

We use our minds to be calm. And that's like learning how to move, only in reverse.

Meditation is the traditional form of Mindfulness. Only instead of waiting until we're in a secluded corner, or on the distant mountain, we practise it as we are, where we are.

Concentration, focus, mesmerism, awareness, mindfulness, are all variations of meditation.

It's about lazering your mind onto a word, a moment, a sound, an action, anything, or event, which consumes your attention to the exclusion of all else.

Frank Zane, the bodybuilder of the 60's, was a fan of meditation, and believed he meditated every time he worked in the gym'. His style was precise, tight and right, for what he wanted to achieve, a form of muscular choreography in which he directed his activity to the goal he had in mind.

It's about hitting what's called the zone. That's meditation. You don't have to be in the corner, on your head. You can learn to do this anywhere, anytime, any way that suits you.

Sir Jackie Stewart did it in the Tyrrell, at 180mph down the Kemmel Straight at Spa.

Rugby players can hit it for parts of a game, where they run, duck, dodge and weave, suffer bone-crushing tackles, and are oblivious to the hits, the pain, the physical effort, simply because there is no effort, it's all part of their being for that duration.

I know of a hurler, who, at the centre of an arena, with over 80,000 people roaring in at him, heard only the smack of the ball on hurls throughout a whole game.

But let's stop there. You don't have to be a formula 1 driver, a Rugby International, or an All-Ireland hurler to experience the bliss and the benefits of meditation.

It's an integral part of the make-up of nearly every human being. And, like most natural skills, it can be learned.

The benefits are beyond words. You can learn how to quiet the wayward mind, relax the tense, uncomfortable body, soothe the tired nerves. You can create the conditions for natural rest, perhaps the most overlooked element in any fitness or wellness programme.

So, maybe it's time to be a bit Mindful, a little bit aware, conscious of just being, quietly, calmly, comfortably, in mind and body.

It's no mystery, no deep secret, nothing as obscure as it's made out to be

Ride The Storm...

He knew the techniques. His product was the best on the market. And he knew that too.

The company's service was first class and acknowledged. Customers were very satisfied. They testified willingly and eloquently about their experience of him and his colleagues.

He presented well, no jargon, no affectation. He liked and respected his customers. And this was reciprocated.

Yet, on this occasion, he found himself struggling, hesitant, even a bit uneasy.

The meeting, requested by a satisfied client with a view to upgrading, had become ragged, disjointed, needing all his skill and determination to keep it on an even keel.

In spite of his difficulties, the event concluded successfully. But it could just as easily have gone awry. When we met, he had mixed feelings about his performance; encouraged by his own tenacity, concerned by the near disaster.

He is honest when he assesses his performance. Life is a daily dose. It needs daily appraisal. Nothing is certain. Which is why he works on himself as much as he does his business.

He knows that he is the instrument of his own performance, and no matter how well the business is on point, he is the epicenter of how it all works.

If he's a bit off, a bit tired, out of form, the whole is out of tune and off song.

He needs to be in the right frame of mind, physically well, and personally set up for the task at hand.

Hence his concern. He saw, on analysis, that his performance, in this particular event, was heroic, that the outcome was the result of previous preparation, diligence, the shaping of an attitude that allowed him resurrect resources that could have been overwhelmed by the unexpected.

Had he been less prepared, unaware, not firing on all cylinders, there might have been dire consequences.

But because he had learned, drilled, practised and repeated his system till he couldn't do it wrong, when the storm broke, though the ship shuddered, he was able to hold the tiller steady and keep on course.

He adapted to the course, worked with the elements, and rode it out.

He put his survival down to being alert to his own response, and how he could best use himself.

That's what being Mindfully Aware can do for you.

It's a skill, a learnable, practical skill. The fundamentals, when you open yourself to them, allow you shift perspective, alter the viewpoint, change perception.

This makes for other choices, options.

The Mind/Body/Mind Effect is of this age.

It's a way of seeing. It brings flexibility to thoughts and actions, offers different decisions. Most people find it helps them use personal abilities and resources. They feel they have more influence in the direction of their lives.

To this end, it pays to halt, come to a stop, check the signs, see if they're pointing to the destination you have in your mind, and in your heart.

And if your actions aren't supporting your aims, change them.

What Elvis Didn't Know...

"Got a Lot o' Livin' to do", sang Elvis in 1956. I remember it well.

For a few years, he really held it all together, the success, the fame, the wealth.

Then it began to unravel and ended in his tragic, and apparently unnecessary, death. Of course, we don't know what else was going on in that man's life, but it seemed as if his death was a direct result of activities that had nothing to do with style, but rather, lifestyle. It appears as if he lost the plot somewhere along the way, and succumbed to the effects of his distractions.

And there indeed, but for the grace of whoever your God may be, go any one of us.

Why mull on this?

Here's why; life tends to reflect how we look at it.

This has been vividly illustrated over the past decade, where accomplished, energetic, creative people, confronted by the despair of no future, no way out, no hope, took those final fatal steps that may none of us ever have to contemplate.

And therefore, vigilance of attitude, in any life, is one of the most vital aspects of being fit, healthy and well.

"A healthy mind in a healthy body" may well be a cliché. It's true. Which is why it's a cliché.

That's why being fit is all about being *well*. It's more than just carbs, protein and six packs.

It's a mindset, a system of belief, thinking, feeling and doing. It's a system of being.

And it's simple enough. Not easy, simple.

What Do You Do With Your Mind When You're Not Using It...?

This is one of the relevant questions today. When we're not conscious in what we're doing, our minds get free rein, and take us where they want. Unless we rein them in.

Car journeys, conversations, day to day matters, can get lost in the fog of routine inattention that leaves them as blank spaces in the day.

'He was elsewhere', 'He was away on his own', 'He wasn't with it', are common observations about any of us that can be justifiably made. We call it preoccupation, or daydreaming, or simply being inattentive.

And whenever it happens, as it does to everyone, it can lay our minds open to whatever thought, idea, association, memory, that may be flitting through it at that moment.

Which is why we need to be mindful. Mindfulness is being aware. It's being conscious of the thoughts, notions, that are in our minds at any given time, and the key is to see the thought as the entity of the moment.

It'll change quickly. Another distraction may come in. Or someone addresses us. Or the phone rings. Or we become aware that we're not doing what we set out to do, and that we've let our minds wander.

Ring a bell?

This kind of distracted attention can become a habit. But it can be addressed.

Inattention isn't a disease. It can be changed, improved, altered completely. It starts with Awareness.

Bannister's Belief..

In 1954, Roger Bannister, Christopher Chataway and Christopher Brasher, broke the perception of human limitations when, after a training campaign in which they analyzed, dissected and performed to their own beliefs and will, succeeded in breaking the four-mi- nute mile.

Up to then, the sub four-minute mile was considered by many to be a myth, something to which humans would aspire, but probably never attain. The trio, along with others who thought as they did, were well known for their athletic prowess. they were advised, warned even, by their elders, and many of their peers, that they would do themselves irreparable damage as a result of their efforts.

They were cautioned about bursting lungs, exploding hearts, ripping muscles, tearing tendons, sundering ligaments.

But with intensive interval training, sprinting techniques, and an innovative running style, they developed a system that helped them achieve their goal.

On May 6th, 1954, a race was staged in which the trio decided that it just might be possible to run the mile in under 4 minutes.

Brasher took the lead, and following him, Bannister, impatient and thinking the pace wasn't up to the level needed, urged him to speed it up. But Brasher kept to the GamePlan and held steady. After the halfway mark, Chataway moved ahead, leading Bannister now into the fourth and final quarter, at which point Bannister let loose, tore into the lead, and with his lungs sucking fire, breasted the tape in 3 minutes, 59.4 seconds.

A record of athletic performance was set, but more significantly, a psychological barrier was broken. What was once considered impossible was soon to become a standard.

Over the next 12 months, 38 sub four minute miles were recorded.

In the late fifties, and through the sixties, four minutes became the aim of every serious miler.

Now, of course the time had probably come for the four minute mile to be broken anyway, and it's possible that a few other athletes would have achieved it in that season, but it was the unshakable belief of Bannister in his own ability, that inspired others to seriously emulate his example and go and do it.

And what's important is this; we can let our doubts become stronger than our beliefs, and thus be overwhelmed by the doubt. Had Bannister listened to the waves of advice, and had he let himself be affected by the paucity of assistance, he certainly wouldn't have achieved the feat he did.

Given the dire performances he had put in to the 1952 Olympics, and the subsequent vilification he received from the press and the public alike, his belief and determination were indeed extraordinary.

It must be said that his achievement was a fitting answer, and a stirring testimony to the strength of his belief and character.

The Significance of Belief.

Our beliefs are fundamental to our daily existence.

See this: **What we believe in,**

Influences

How we think,

Influences

How we feel,

Influences

How we behave/act/react/ respond/ perform/live.

It's an interesting model, isn't it?

It pretty well applies to anything. It also indicates the force of basic beliefs we may still have, long forgotten, unacknowledged, but driving us daily in our decisions and reactions.

What we believe in tends to dominate how we use ourselves in life.

There are talented people who have no belief in their ability to do what they're capable of.

They will see the obstacles they encounter as proof of their belief.

Their thinking is in the form of doubt, and they succumb.

We've all experienced it at some time or other.

Shakespeare put it succinctly; 'Our doubts are traitors and make us lose the good we oft might gain, by fearing to attempt.'

Then, there are determined individuals who have total belief in their ability to get things done, achieve aims, overcome obstacles, do whatever is necessary to get to a goal.

Their belief opens possibilities where others only see the obstacle.

Their thinking is in the form of belief, which brings everything into the realm of possibility.

That's no guarantee of course that they're going to succeed.

But whatever chance we have with an attitude of belief, we don't even get on the pitch with an attitude of doubt.

One point; try not to confuse positive thinking, and its effect on possibility, with the notion that because we choose to see what we *want* to see, *regardless* of facts, that that's the way to go.

There is a clear difference between *examining* facts, and seeing possibilities, and rushing in regardless of the facts, and reacting to wishful thinking.

The Biology of Belief...

Thoughts influence feelings.

Feelings direct actions.

That's why the best psychologists, psychiatrists, coaches, psychotherapists and motivators in any field talk about the *skill* of thinking.

It's a habit.

Like any skill, it has its fundamentals and can be learned, developed, changed, improved, made more creative, shaped, and inclined in any direction.

The mind is a potent source of creativity. Being mindfully aware of what's going on between our ears is a skill very well worth developing. This is being Mindfully Aware of how we use that powerhouse.

This is what allows us decide what our minds do, either *to* us , or *for* us. (Excepting illness).

No computer ever has, does, or will be able to do that. As humans, it's our privilege to be able to do our own programming.

Those who understand this know the power and the use of it in their lives. But like any kind of instrument, it's as good as the use to which it's put. It's a decisive factor in any endeavor, to be well, to achieve, to succeed, or simply to be, in any life.

The Skill for a Happy Life...

With Christmas over, there are a lot of stories of excess, and the consequences.

Too much food, too much drink, too many late and boisterous nights, too many lazy days, a general stagnation in the rhythm of life, all take a toll.

But, it's easily and quickly remedied.

With a couple of well-planned goals, a sound mind-set, a practical application, we can arrest and reverse these effects quickly. The mind and body are powerful allies in the quest for a long, happy and a healthy life.

Most of us have useful advantages here. We just need to use them.

Start with the mind. Revisit this upstairs power-zone. Let yourself think about what makes your life worthwhile.

What's of vital concern to you? What makes you glad to open your eyes in the morning, feel grateful for this next day, that life's ok, maybe even better than ok, feel, hear, see, with that zing of vitality?

When was the last time you felt that? What caused it? How can you resurrect it?

That's your privilege.

It's not some vague, woolly, touchy-feely soft-headed notion. But think of a moment, and event, an incident in life that means a lot to you, some event, however big or small, that you have in your life that moved you then, and moves you now. And treasure it.

Science is daily proving that what we believed all along about the connection of the mind and the body to be right; the thoughts you choose affect every single cell in your body.

Daily, we experience in our bodies, how we choose to think in our minds.(Yes, I know there are people who do not have the faculty of thought selection. So, if you're not one of those people, rejoice in that fact and apply yourself with gratitude.)

Dwell on that comforting thought over the weekend

Where Are You Going...?

Sorry to read of Peter Sarstedt's passing the other day. He wrote and sang 'where Do You Go To , My Lovely', in the sixties. It became a kind of anthem for the mores of the time.

After a brief reflection on the times, and a few times in particular, it instigated a few questions for myself, which I thought I'd share with you.

Where do *you* want to go?

Where ever it is, you need to know what your destination is, or at least your *intended* destination.

Otherwise your journey can take you in circles, up the wrong roads, into unknown quarters; anywhere but where you want to be.

That goes as much for life as it does for a daytrip.

So, where ever you want to go, make a written note to yourself. Keep referring to it.

All the time.

Quite a few people regard this as stupid; a simplistic exercise for the less intelligently endowed, the sort of exercise that should be done by dummies who can't see in their minds the glorious, golden, dazzling destination that entices the eye, molds the mind, and summons the senses.

Write descriptively to yourself where you want to go. Describe the landscape of your imagination. Draw the dreams you dare to entertain. Hop on the horse of Higher Humanity. Go galloping to your Goals.

And have a good life on the way.

Mind Your Own Business...

In the world of business today, there is huge emphasis placed on the technology involved. This is especially so in the matter of communication; we're told that unless we're on Facebook, Twitter, and the plethora of other social media outlets, that our lives will come to a halt and we'll be history.

It's interesting that among the number of some truly successful operators I've been dealing with over the years, all have been firm advocates of personal contact; phone, letter, and most emphatically, face-to-face. This came up because I'd asked a few people what their feelings were about their achievements. Specifically, I asked them if there was a factor that they felt was prominent, that I might mention to other people in business, and especially to people starting out.

The first and *most prominent* point they made was the value of a sense of purpose and the importance of relationships and personal contact.

All business, relationships, projects, in any field, are mostly reliant on people.

Now, while some initial contact, or referrals, may have been instigated on the internet, the vital element in any transaction thereafter, was to write to or speak with the individuals involved.

Which is why it is necessary for all of us, large, medium, small enterprises, to be aware of the value of our personal communication habits.

What we believe in, how we think, how we feel about what we do, and with whom we deal, is what determines the value of our communication.

Regardless of the enterprise or project, WE are the instruments with which we create our performance.

It means keeping that instrument in tune, on song, and well-conditioned.

And that's a skill we all need to learn, practice, and develop.

This is a great time of year to put a system in place.

There is Only One thing To Do...

Whatever you do for yourself in the coming year, there is only one way to get it going.

We all have choices to make. Every day. That's what freedom is; being able to choose.

Perhaps we could take a moment, reflect, on some time when we were at the mercy of circumstances, or the doings of others. And what we were aware of, more than anything else, would have been the feeling of helplessness, the constraint of being held in a position which we felt we couldn't even remotely influence.

But even then, we have a choice; we can decide how to feel about it. That's what got a lot of the unfortunates through WW11 when they were flung into concentration camps. Or on to battlefields about which they had no belief.

But our choice isn't as stark as that.

Our biggest problem can be what we'll watch on TV, whether we'll have wine with dinner, or where to go on holiday.

And that is not to denigrate wine, TV, or holidays.

But when we take a view that we are so fortunate to have that kind of choice to see as a dilemma, maybe it's time for us to re-assess our good fortune and make the most of what opportunities and advantages are available to us.

And we may well find ourselves doing what we previously saw as a tough option, a less comfortable way to go, or a less popular one, *but the one we know to be the right one.*

Everything, everything, starts with a choice and a decision, and if we want to get to a destination, there is only one thing to do; start the journey.

Now.

Action...for the coming year....

Until we decide to do something, nothing ever happens for us.

Ever.

To be indecisive is to capitulate. You may even decide to do nothing. Which is a decision.

And it's ours.

This is the gift of the human mind. Some, due to regrettable decisions, would say it's the curse of the human mind. And that's a pity, because that indicates a surrender to the consequences of previous decisions, that's all.

It's good to acknowledge mistakes. It's even better to remind ourselves that we can still make new decisions, open new possibilities, make new lives.

This thinking delivers mistakes, poor decisions, wrong turnings, into a learning process.

This reinstates the freedom of choice, the power of decision, into our lives. It helps give meaning and direction to our days.

May you choose wisely, and decide strongly, in the coming year.

Bright New Beginnings...

Sense of purpose seems to flow into our lives at this time of year; New Year, Fresh Start, New Beginnings.

As a custom, it gets a lot of ridicule and disparagement. And that's a pity, because if you feel the New Year is a time when you'd like to start something, put a plan into action, follow an idea, then do it.

Just because you'll hit a hurdle or two doesn't mean New Year Resolutions don't work.

All it means is that you've hit a hurdle, and whether you started on the First of January, or the Tenth of May, you'd probably hit a hurdle anyway.

And that's where you, as your own person, can decide whether your resolution is worthy or not.

Try this.

Write down two things you'd like to get done this year. They don't have to shake the Earth or turn the World into a Fountain of Peace(Fat Chance) overnight.

But they can be two things that'll make a difference to you, or to something else, or someone else, that you know will make your world, or theirs, that bit better, or maybe just a bit less bad.

Once you've decided, take it on and put the action into it. Don't ask for agreement or approval. Just start it and keep on taking the simple steps.

Then it can't not happen.

Have a wonderful New Year.

Would You Agree…?

"It is a lesson which all history teaches wise men, to put trust in ideas, and not in circumstances."

Ralph Waldo Emerson

1803-1882, Poet and Essayist

"In essence, if we want to direct our lives, we must take control of our consistent actions. It's not what we do occasionally that shapes our lives, but what we do consistently."

Tony Robbins Author and Speaker

Constant Energy, Unwavering Concentration.

Robust Health is largely a decision, your decision.

Unless you're clinically ill, you've a means, wherever you are, and more, a duty, to yourself, others in your life, and to any undertaking in which you take part, to keep yourself well, healthy and fit.

The means are simple, available to anyone.

But they need to be applied and practised.

Then they work. In fact, they can't not work.

HERE'S A THOUGHT.....Vitality shows in not only the ability to persist, but the ability to start over.

F. Scott Fitzgerald

This is what attitude is about. The Americans have a great tradition of getting up after a fall, dusting themselves off, and starting all over again.

They talk about it, think about it, they even sing about it.

But most of all, they practise it.

SEE THIS... Success sometimes seems to be about hanging on after others have let go.

Or, as Rudyard Kipling put it, so well, "If you can force your heart and nerve and sinew,

To serve you one more turn, long after they have gone,

And so, hold on when there is nothing in you,

Except the will, that says to them, hold on."

Consider This.....A little knowledge that acts, is worth infinitely more than a lot of knowledge that is idle.

The Clear Advantage...

Most people agree that it's an advantage to have a clear mind when undertaking a task.

Sir Jackie Stewart, former World Champion racing driver, is emphatic about this. He believed that any race he won, was won in the first five laps, when his mind was where it needed to be.

While competitors were jockeying, shunting, darting for position, he took a clear path, preplanned, and drove his own race.

It applies to anything. Be clear on where you're going, know how to get there, take decisive action.

One of the benefits of practising one of the forms of Mindful Awareness is having a clear mind.

It's a simple enough skill, when you know how.

There's a whole book written on this by Matthew Syed. The title is 'Bounce', appropriately enough, as he's a former International Table Tennis Champion.

The subtitle, though, is far more indicative; 'The Myth of Talent, and The Power of Practice'.

In any undertaking, the key is having that basic knowledge, and practising till you get it right, or as Tony Buzan says, till you can't get it wrong.

Keep it simple. And Do It.

The Mindful Edge...

Sometimes, it does a body good to just BE, to stop, take a break, listen to the tick of the clock, the drone of distant traffic, the quiet that lies within.

We need something other than the peremptory should do, must do, ought to do, must.

And just BE.

The world still spins.

Life goes on.

Time passes.

The mind stills.

Emotions calm.

And we get a rest from the relentless imperative.

Then we can rejoin, at pace, at choice.

It's a skill. So practice it.

Ignite The Coming Month;

Every morning, do your stretches, open your lungs to a couple of deep breaths, and decide on a direction; then start your day.

Do it every morning. Got that? Every morning.

Watch what happens over a month.

Get started on it today, and I'll show you why this system changes things, events, viewpoints, over time.

When you create an attitude of helpfulness, will, determination and goodwill, it does more than shine a light on your life and your aims.

It forms connection points to opportunities, directions, areas, and people, that may have been there before, but weren't seen

Three Things You Need to Know: (again)...

1

You are how you breathe.

Oxygen is regarded by many nutritionists now as the First Nutrient.

Your regular, day-to-day breathing has a profound effect on your health.

Breathe deeply, slowly and often, feeling the whole upper body move as you bring the respiratory muscles into play.

2

You are, or should be, 65% water. This percentage lets your body metabolism, and your methylation, work as Nature intended.

If you're not, it can't.

3

You are indeed what you eat.

Your food can help the health of the cells that go to make up your body.

Every part of you is composed of cells.

Nourish the cells, feed them well, with the right nutrients, and it will be physically impossible for your body not to respond positively.

Got that? Three things. Read them again.

Repeat them every morning for the next week.

Learn them. And use them.

Good luck.

What's Your Excuse...?

When a car needs a service, you know it, because it stutters, jumps, falters and drags.

Starting's hard. There's no power. Performance is sluggish. It's as if the car has a mind of its own and expresses a resentment at even the thought of getting up and going.

It's like the get up and go, has got up and gone.

Ring a bell?

It's much the same with us, isn't it?

We falter, stab and stumble over things we should be annihilating.

There's nothing wrong with us. It's more like something's not quite right with us.

But we can do something about that.

We can, like the well-cared-for, well-serviced car, have power, energy, speed and lasting stamina.

Thousands of people, with whom I've been privileged to work over the last 50 years, have learned how.

They're the ones who've learned, practised, and applied the habits for a rewarding life.

They're skills. They can be learned. Then practised. Then used. That's all. Simple as that.

Not always easy. But certainly simple.

The practicing is the fundamental requirement, and the foundation, for boundless energy, lazer-like concentration, and life-long health and vitality

For the Coming Week...

For the first year of our lives, we were on our knees, back, or sides. We were horizontal.

Then we started to learn how to walk. And that was a tough course. We fell a lot. We got up. Fell again. Got up again.

Then we learned a few tricks; hold a table edge, a low chair, a parental leg. We persisted. In a few weeks we were putting a few steps together, getting there. Then we added a few more. We were walking. Despite the falls, trips, discouragements, impediments, we were walking.

In a few short months, we had to be told to stop running, sit down, make less noise and behave ourselves.

There are a couple of lessons in that experience.

We had a clear aim, our belief was total, and the determination never faltered.

We were inspired, persistent, decided.

We never lost sight of the aim.

And we succeeded.

What, or who, do you think, would inspire you now?

Are you willing to persist? To continue fighting in the face of adversity, discouragement, ridicule, dismissal, rejection?

Are you decided? Another word we could use is for decided is determined.

We determine our lives by the decisions we take.

Look at the three underlined questions. Spend a bit, or even a lot, of time on them.

Answer them to yourself, *not* anyone else.

The Curse of Tyranny...

If you've ever faced a tyranny, you know what it is to be free.
D.N.H.

Essential Exercise...

You don't need fanaticism. Indeed, you're better without it.

But you do need discipline. Not a huge amount, but enough to get you started on a regular basis, to get you out of bed, out of the comfy settee, out the front door. Or to the gym. Or over the fields.

Whatever it is that's exercise to you.

It needs regularity. Not massive exertion.

The muscles need to moved, exerted, pushed a bit, so you pant, run a bit short of breath.

That makes your heart work, your lungs open, your blood pulse round the body and revitalize every muscle, tissue, organ in your system.

Then you feel better, you think better, you eat better, you sleep better, you work better, you play better.

You live better.

REGULARITY is the way.

STARTING is the key..

Decide Your Own Day....

"I will waste not even a precious second today in anger or petty hate or small minded jealousy .

I know that the seeds I sow I will harvest, because every action, good or bad, is always followed by an equal reaction.

I will plant only good seeds this day."

Og Mandino

Small Change, Big Difference...

What makes the difference to the results you get?

Minor alterations, small improvements, little switches.

And they all add up to a huge difference.

It's good mental discipline, a mental exercise. And that's how it works, as a neuro-muscular skill.

The focusing on the positive activity in search of a positive outcome, creates a positive state of expectation.

This has the happy effect of spilling over into daily life, improving posture, breathing patterns, and the necessary self- esteem for day -to -day living.

This has a positive effect, on the mind, the body, the nervous system.

It enhances life immeasurably.

It will trim you down, tone you up, and resurrect energy you never knew you had.

So, learn it well, and PRACTISE.

Choice of Thought...

In his 19th century Journals, Ralph Waldo Emerson wrote, *"Life consists of what a man is thinking of all day."*

If we continue to think like we've always thought, we'll continue to get what we've always got.

Our daily thought, and choices translate into our daily actions.

Our actions accumulate to form our habits.

Our habits form our character.

Our character attracts our circumstances.

Our circumstances determine our future ...

Taking responsibility for our choices starts *with choosing our thoughts.*

Courage...

Talking with a woman the other day, I witnessed an instance of pure courage.

She'd just come from the bank. The manager had told her that her overdraft facility was being curtailed, and that if it exceeded the limit by a cent, one cent, it would be withdrawn and the balance put into a personal loan. Immediately

This was delivered in a tone and language to match the authority and officialdom with which it was intended.

I'd first met this woman in 2007. She'd had 45 people in employment then. She now ran a lean operation employing 3 people.

She had moved premises too, from a prime location to a lesser-known, some would say obscure, place.

Her work is related to the clothing/fashion/media/image industries, so much so that many in her line mistake the façade for the substance.

Her own life she described as having an intrigue of its own; her husband had gone off with another, not another woman, a man, her son had run up a debt which necessitated his hasty departure to foreign parts, and for which she was now being held responsible. The sale of what had been her family home would just about cover her liabilities, including the son's. She'd have nothing but would be in the clear; debt free.

She saw this as a great opportunity. It was her starting point, a place from which she could bring her know-how, her imagination, her determination, to the game.

She had outlined roughly her intentions, how she would use her own personal abilities to bring about her goal. She was very clear about this.

A quietly spoken and discreet woman, she nevertheless recognized her own qualities of courage, determination and perseverance, and the ability to heed her own counsel, not to be thrown off by the naysayers, the constraints of convention, nor the fear of uncertainty.

The conversation was simply a declaration of belief, a statement of earnest intent.

I'm sure that, like me, you'll be wishing her well, and that she achieves the success she so richly deserves.

How to Stay Motivated...

A shot of motivation, once a month, is like doing an exercise session, once a month; it'll have some kind of effect in that you'll be aware of the use of it, but you won't get fit, preserve your health, or improve your strength.

Some will say, 'Well, it's better than nothing.' And they'd be right. It is.

But that's it. It'll keep the point in your mind, but it won't do you much good beyond that.

The key to success in exercise is regularity. Some do much and often, some do little and often.

What's important is the 'often'.

That's why motivation is a daily practice. Even a few moments, every day, can establish an idea, allow it to grow, develop a strategy, let it develop, so that it begins to crystallize into a clearly identified aim, something you may want to do, or achieve, or become.

Just let it happen.

Integrity...

Do what you feel in your heart to be right…..

you'll be criticized anyway.

Motivated...?

There's a great deal of talk about motivation. And it's good to be motivated. But it's not the only answer.

Here's why.

To do anything, or get anything done, something must be started.

You can be motivated to think about doing something.

And you can be motivated to feel strongly about something.

You can be even motivated to start acting on something.

But to get through the start, get to the middle, and then to the finish, takes discipline, will, determination, resolve.

They have their fundamentals too. And they're as learnable as any other skill.

How's your will?

Are you resolute?

Determined?

Do you use the discipline to exploit these great qualities?

Small Changes, Big Difference...

It rarely happens quickly. Changes take place with apparent slowness, and then tumble into existence as if they came overnight.

There's a whole new scientific study called 'Systems Based Science'.

It deals with how apparently insignificant elements can be in existence for a while, and as they ally themselves to each other, can be transformed into a formidable force.

This can be applied to any condition in Life. See how a healthy person can begin to have a few beers on a weeknight, then begin to have the odd cigarette, then go to the restaurant after closing time, then eat a Full Irish to mollify the hangover.

Within six months, the habit becomes more intrusive, and a healthy human becomes overweight, fatigued, run down and unhealthy.

It works the other way too. Someone cuts his drinking to Saturday night only, cuts down, or out, on tobacco use, starts walking every night during the week, and one of the weekend days, learns how to breathe well, and in three months has lost weight, feels better, and can't believe how he's performing in work.

I see that all the time.

This isn't new though. We're all familiar with the saying, 'Little and often', 'Rome wasn't built in a day', 'Make haste slowly', and similar bon mots that identify the power of persistence.

It's good to remember that we can exert considerable change by simple means, doing things well, consistently, and with a bit of a will.

So, make the small changes, commit to yourself, and get it done.

The Real Fear...The Fear of Success...

The greatest fear is not that we may be inadequate, but that we can succeed outrageously, and the responsibility and commitment that that success can bring.

Playing small doesn't serve anyone. There's nothing useful in thinking like that just because others won't feel insecure.

We, all of us, were born to a purpose in life.

When we honour that purpose, we liberate ourselves and those around us.

The End in Mind...

Profound commitment to a dream does not confine or constrain: it liberates. Even a difficult, winding path can lead to your goal **if youfollow it to the end.**

~Paul Coelho

On This Day...

A time ago, I posed a question on how you felt about your potential.

The interesting, and revealing, thing was that there were so many people who had not thought about it before.

What they HAD thought about though, was what they had in mind as goals, aims, aspirations.

The difference is that goals demand a plan, a state of action, and a direction.

Potential is a personal value that we bring to that process.

Potential is what exercises our capacity for achievement, what we often discover in times of trial or crisis, when we find we're much more than we thought we were.

Potential Awareness brings the force of thought to the plans, the action, the direction we take.

Think about this. Then ask yourself again; how do you feel, *really feel*, about your potential?

Mind Reading...

Few people can read minds. I don't know anyone who can.

Yet we tend to think that those near and dear to us 'know' that they matter.

Maybe they don't. Or maybe they've forgotten because it's been so long since we let them know.

So, it might be a good thing to remind them.

This weekend.

It doesn't have to be a splurge, or an extravagance.

A simple statement, a personal gesture, a true compliment, does the giver and the recipient a lot of good.

Today...

Today is important. Today is more important than any other day.

What you do, say, experience today will be part of your life, for the rest of your life.

That goes for every day.

But today is the only one you can do anything about, today.

Get to it.

Quick Question...

Before you answer it, get a pen and paper.

Then write your answers to the following *three* questions.

You're only answering one at a time.

And they're all quick; Though you mightn't find the answers that quick.

So, try it.

What does fitness mean to you?

How do you feel, really feel, about your potential?

What do you feel you're *getting* from your own potential?

You can interpret these questions any way that suits *you*. There's no wrong or right answer.

Spend time on this. Use a lunch hour, or some ten or fifteen minute gap in your day, to answer your questions, to yourself, *for* yourself.

You'll find that though the questions are quick, the answers aren't.

The Mind/Body Principle...

Research over the past decades has shown that the mind and the body are inextricably linked. It's been acknowledged over the centuries, but now science appears to be confirming what we've believed all along.

They affect each other every moment of the day. This can work horribly against us, or powerfully for us.

Professor Bruce Lipton, in his book, '*The Biology of Belief*', explains how the 50 to 70 trillion cells in our bodies are affected by intention, belief, perception.

We've all experienced that phenomenon.

Sometimes it's been the effects of fear, or dismay, or disappointment. We've been physically sickened by some event, a betrayal, the loss of a friendship, the cut of a remark.

Or we may be uplifted by encouragement during a time of hardship, when a kind word has opened up some possibility, or we realise that we can do something about our dilemma, or we get a surge of courage and revitalisation in some instance.

We not only understand the experience intellectually; *we experience it physically.*

What we need to realise as well is that those experiences, good or bad, stem from how *we decide* to view a circumstance.

So, when we speak about talking ourselves into being spectacularly indecisive, we begin to see the effects of suggestion, conditioning, perception.

Current research is supporting the view that we have much more influence over our circumstances, events, lives, than we've ever believed.

And there's the word; 'believed'.

When we believe we're procrastinators, that's what we become. And the more we tell ourselves we are, the better we get at it.

Change that viewpoint.

Alter the possibility in your mind.

Start with that decision.

Then implement it. Practise it. Get good at THAT.

Then stay with your intention.

Effective Procrastination...

Procrastination is one of the topics that bedevil so many people you'd think they'd have discovered a cure for it by now.

Yet, there are no educational modules in courses I've researched that deal with it.

My belief is that it's regarded as a universal malady that effects everyone from Obama to O'Hagan.

What most people don't see is that it's a decision. It's a decision to not do, what we know we need to do, to get where we want to go.

And we've learned very well to reinforce it in our lives. We're exceptionally good at it.

We say, 'My problem is procrastination'.

And we say it to ourselves, to our colleagues, to our friends, to anyone who'll listen. And we say it with such conviction, a certitude bordering on enthusiasm, that it's impossible not to be affected, infected, and seriously influenced by how we express ourselves.

So, here's a suggestion.

Remove the problem.

Change the statement. ,

Alter the belief. Actively.

With purpose.

With intent. Say, "I don't hang around. I get things done.",
or, "I'm a doer."!

Open your mind to the possibility of change.

Start implementing it. Do it in small ways, big ways,
whatever-suits-you ways.

And don't procrastinate.

Do it now.

Fit for Purpose...

To want to get fit is a fine thing.

It's even better when you take action on it. And it's a simple thing to do. Not always easy, but simple.

You decide, start doing it, stay at it, evaluate, adjust, and keep doing it.

Couldn't be simpler. So go to it.

But know this; fitness is just one component of being well.

And it's vital to be well. A lot of people are not ill, but neither are they really well.

And there's more to being well than not being ill.

Wellness is a physical, psychological, emotional, and intentional state of existence.

And, like fitness, notwithstanding clinical illness, is simply achieved.

It's a skill. Like all skills, it has its fundamentals. And they can be learned.

By anyone.

Hope...

Hope is to Life as Oxygen is to the blood.

Feed on both.

Have a great weekend

The Spirit Moves.

There's much talk about 'motivation' in business today...

And there's equal talk about the value of logic and the danger of emotion...

there's an ambiguity involved here.....

to be motivated is to be moved...........

that means being driven by emotion, and many people think that emotion has no place in business.....

But that's what being motivated is...

'I Didn't Mean That...'

'I didn't mean that...', 'That's not what I meant...', 'What I meant was...'.

Sound familiar? We all do it, don't we? Sometimes, to make our point, we scramble out the first available words, and miscommunicate.

Try this daily.

What is it you intend for you, your actions, your expression, your words, your relationships, your life?

What do you really intend? How can you find your intentions? How can you use them, put them into action?

How can you manage your day, yourself, your abilities, your environment, to include opportunities that will bring you nearer to your intentions?

If you could do this, would you? If so, when?

You can apply this to anything. For example, how can you make a pleasantly memorable weekend, for yourself, and for those near and dear?

Go out of your way to do a small act of thoughtfulness, say a word of encouragement, express a bit of appreciation. And then forget about it, you're not looking for recognition, or praise, or even acknowledgement.

Just deliver a scrap of kindness. And then shut up about it.

Pay attention to your intention. And make a great couple of days for yourself and others in your life.

How to Succeed at Anything...

Whatever needs to be done, and that can be anything from getting out of bed on time, to creating a magni-ficent achievement in your life, to just getting through the day, or coping with the impossible, many people who have achieved their aim did it by doing this;

Take a Decision.

Do it With a Will.

See it Through.

Start with that thought, and let it pervade and guide your day.

A Painful Decision...

A student of mine told me about a decision she took recently. As she spoke, it struck me how we need to be aware of the faculties of Reason and Emotion.

She decided to do something she didn't want to do, but knew she needed to do. And that takes courage, determination.

Often, because of the strength of feeling we have about our beliefs, tenets, persuasions, we find it very difficult to acknowledge that a different idea may be more true, or more practical, or more fair, or more useful, than the one we've followed for years, even decades.

And a decision to which we need to commit, often requires us to challenge our own beliefs, consent to a new perspective, accede to the virtue of another viewpoint.

Hence the possible pain. We're admitting that we were wrong, that someone else knows better, that we don't have all the answers, that we're human, fallible, imperfect, mortal.

But we're also saying we're open-minded, tolerant, ready to learn, capable of improving, approachable, reasonable.

Which brings us back to the faculties; Reason and Emotion.

The lady's decision was painful because she had to dig in, find the courage to acknowledge the significance of it, and because that was her heartfelt belief, be big enough to swallow her pride and assent to what needed to be done.

Now there's integrity for you.

Be true to yourself. Have a great week.

Powerful Health Weapon...

Do this at odd moments during the day. Every day.

It takes about 40 seconds. Maximum. Done 10 times a day, that's 6 minutes and 40 seconds.

Which leaves you 23hours, 53 minutes, and 20 seconds to spend how you like.

Sit, or stand, comfortably straight.

Breathe in slowly, through your nose.

Exhale slowly, through your nose.

Observe your stomach muscle movements. Let them in and out naturally as you breathe.

Relax.

Let it happen.

Bit by gentle bit, let the whole upper body come into the movement.

Slowly, smoothly, rhythmically, let the breathing deepen, the lungs fill, the whole upper body become involved in the gentle and steady inhalation and exhalation.

Use your mind to observe, correct, guide and develop this natural ability.

Think about it. Let the mind and the body work on it together.

The rhythm of the breathing will bring a sequence of activity into place that allows the nerves, the muscles, the mind and the entire system rest, relax and refresh.

It cleans the system, rests the mind, and revitalises every cell in your body.

It converts your food into energy and body tissue.

It carries away the wastes and the toxins.

It clears the mind.

Forty seconds a time. Ten times a day. Do this for 28 days. See what happens.

Choosing Our Thoughts

"We always have choices.

We can install any thought in our minds.

We can remove any thought from our minds.

When we are indiscriminate in our choice of thoughts, the actions that follow may have unfavourable consequences.

When we choose thoughts that complement our aims, the likely actions that follow may very well result in favourable circumstances."

'No Time to Stand and Stare...'

Here's a pleasant reminder of a time when we all had more of that elusive commodity, time.

Take the time to read it, savour the question, recall it. And even, observe it.

What is this life if, full of care,

We have no time to stand and stare.

No time to stand beneath the boughs

And stare as long as sheep or cows.

No time to see, when woods we pass,

Where squirrels hide their nuts in grass.

No time to see, in broad daylight,

Streams full of stars, like skies at night.

No time to turn at Beauty's glance,

And watch her feet, how they can dance.

No time to wait till her mouth can

Enrich that smile her eyes began.

A poor life this if, full of care,

We have no time to stand and stare.

Discipline is Freedom...

The great advantage, and privilege, of being in the free world, is that we enjoy the freedom of choice.

We can be who we want to be, go where we want to go, do what we want, live how we like, with respect for the rights of others, of course.

We can choose a Destination, learn the journey, the steps to it, and get on with it.

The journey can be life-long, year-long, a few months-long, or, like a detox, 5-days-long.

One of the corollaries, people have found, of doing a detox is that it helps clear the mind as well as the body.

It also impresses hugely on the power of choice. It reinforces the power of discipline and the fact that discipline is a choice, and we have the freedom to apply it. Or not.

This clarifies the freedom and force of Decision, and how, with a bit of will and gumption, we can affect our own lives.

And of course, this spills over into everything else. Confidence, self-belief, creativity in our daily lives, all get a hefty boost.

This opens the door to more choice, the possibilities begin to re-emerge, and that really highlights the Freedom of Discipline.

And that's the key point; Discipline is the route to, and the price of, Freedom.

And Freedom, once achieved, feeds on the discipline of the Free.

Too often it's seen as a constraint.

It's not. It's an opportunity to express ourselves.

Down the centuries, men and women have given their lives for the privilege of that freedom. But like all assets, opportunities, resources, abilities, it's as good as the use to which it's put.

And you can make the choice any day, at any time, at any age

It seems We Really Are What We Eat...

According to the World Health Organisation, 75%, or thereabouts, of all illness, is as a result of malnutrition.

And that's in the Western World. Years ago, a malnutrition advisory group, in England, studied the hospital population in South East England.

That's probably the wealthiest part of England. The hospitals visited were private, which means that the hospital population was one of the wealthiest groups in one of the wealthiest parts of the land.

They found that 66% of the patients were overweight and suffering in varying degrees from malnutrition.

Of that 66%, 50% were in hospital because of malnutrition. That's 33% of the hospital population.

And that was of a relatively small group of hospitals, of the smaller group of better-off people in that country.

Isn't it ironic? One of the wealthiest sections, in one of the wealthiest parts, of one of the wealthiest countries, in the world, a third of the hospital population were there because of malnutrition.

Have a nice weekend.

Do It Anyway.......

Everything doesn't have to be certain before you move forward. As a matter of fact, few things are.

But you can plan, prepare and ready yourself as well as you can, and then move.

Sometimes you'll fall. Sometimes you'll succeed beyond your wildest imaginings.

Circumstances arise, change, develop that you couldn't possibly have foreseen. But the fact that you've prepared puts you in the mindset to try, fight, endure.

And that's often the best kind of preparation we can have.

Have a good week.

A French Tale...

This story takes place in the Auvergne Region, in Central France. It concerns an elderly gentleman I'd met in 1971 in my wife's town, Moulins-sur-Allier, and with whom I'd become friendly. His name was Mr. Jean Gaston. He had been a soldier in the First World War, and a celebrated Resistance fighter in World War Two. He now ran his newsagent's and tobacco shop in the square of the town.

One day, after we'd been acquainted a couple of years, this was 1975, he invited me to accompany him on a visit to a WW2 museum, high in the remoter part of the Auvergne hills.

The following morning, I picked him up at 5.30 am and we set off.

The museum, he told me, was in commemoration of a battle in 1944, between a Resistance group, and three full German battalions. Most of the Resistance group was made up of very young people, and elderly, because all the people of the ages in between, were either in the army, prison camps, or in active Resistance groups around the country.

On the way to the museum, Jean told me to take a turn at some cross-roads. We drove for a short while, till we came to a derelict cottage at which he asked me to stop. We got out of the car, and he continued his story of the battle.

The purpose of the attack by the group back in those days of war, was to delay the Germans in their journey as reinforcements against the impending Allied Invasion.

Having held the might of the soldiers for nearly nine days, the Resistance fighters retreated, scattering in the hilly and difficult countryside. Their losses were high, but they had achieved their aim.

Jean, my friend, had been visiting the site of the battle every year since about 1954. One day, he told me, he took a wrong turning in the labyrinth network of tiny roads that led to the village. He came to a cottage at which a middle-aged man was standing at the gate. The man had a pile of small sticks on top of one of the pillars, and was sharpening them systematically, using a tiny penknife. Jean introduced himself, explained he'd got lost, and said where he wanted to go.

The two men chatted for a while. They were both ex-Resistance fighters, and though they'd never met, had heard of each other, and had mutual friends. Jean thanked the man, Robert Feuillore, and went on his way.

Arriving at the museum, Jean made a note to himself to look for any mention of Robert Feuillore.

What he found, chilled him.

Commander Robert Feuillore had been one of the heroes, who, in the gallant attack that delayed the German advance to Northern France, in May 1944, had been shot to death by the enemy. He was now buried in Vallon-en-Sully, the small village in which he'd been born, beside his wife, Yvette, who had also been killed in that encounter.

On his way back from the museum, Jean went by the road and to the cottage at which he'd met Robert.

When he came to the cottage, what met him was the ruin at which we were both now looking.

The little iron gate was hanging off the hinges. The pathway to the house was overgrown. The front door was ajar, showing a derelict and weathered abandoned interior. Most of the windows were broken. Shards of remaining glass jutting from the frames, letting the sweltering heat of the summers, and the sub-zero cold of the snow and the icy winds, do their worst, in winter.

On one of the gate pillars, though, was the tiny penknife, and the pile of sticks, that Jean had witnessed being used by the man he'd met only hours before. Jean told me he'd picked up the tiny bone-handled knife, put it in his pocket, and got from that place fast.

He looked at me for reaction, lifted his shoulders, and his eyebrows, in Gallic wonder. We got back in the car and drove off. I didn't know what to think.

Every year after that, when we went to Mont Muchet, we drove by the cottage.

Every year we stopped, got out of the car, and just looked. I always had the feeling he was looking for a sign, something to prove that what he'd told me was true, something that would validate his story.

At Easter of 1996, I went as usual to visit Jean's newsagent, but it was no more.

Instead, there was a busy café. Fearing the worst, I went in and made enquiries.

The café was run by Jean's son, Michel. When I said who I was, his face brightened, and he said," Ah yes, the Irishman of whom my father spoke." His face saddened then, and he continued, "My father died just after Christmas this year. He had a peaceful, happy death. And he told me that if you should call, he would like you to have this." And he handed me a small box.

I thanked him, left the shop and made my way to a table on the square. Slowly, I opened the box, having a good idea what I was going to find. And there it was, the little bone-handled penknife.

As I took it out, I wondered, and still wonder to this day, whether I'm the victim, a willing victim, I don't mind saying, of a humorous, imaginative old man whom it was my privilege to have met in this life, or if I'm the witness to a truth so profound and mysterious, that I cannot, nor ever will, even begin to understand it.

Je ne sais pas.

Learning for Life...

The *capacity* to learn is a *gift;*

The *ability* to learn is a *skill;*

The *willingness* to learn is a *choice.*

I thought this notion worthy of a page to itself

The Perfect Excuse ...

'I'm not really ready.'

'It's the wrong time.'

'It's summertime. No one does it at this time of the year.'

'I'll wait till I've thought about it a bit more.'

'This is a busy time, I can't start now.'

'The holidays are coming up, I'd never get it done.'

'I'll do it in the Autumn.'

'...when the kids are back at school.'

'......when the evenings get shorter.'

'.......after the August weekend.'

'.......after the football/hurling season is finished.'

'....when I settle back into a routine.'

'...in October.'

'...after the October weekend.'

'.....November's the perfect month.'

'…it's too close to Christmas.'

'…after the Christmas holidays.'

'….I'll let January get out of the way.'

'…..I'll start in Lent.'

'…..I need to focus for the Easter Quarter.'

'……the very day Easter's over.'

'….when the evenings begin to stretch.'

'…when the weather's a bit warmer.'

'..do it for the holidays.'

'…..it's all a bit hectic, I'll get the holidays done.'

'…..it's summertime. No one starts anything at this time of the year.'

'…when I can't think of any more excuses.'

An Effective Strategy...

If your current habits are not helping you get where you want to go, you need to change your habits, or your destination. Or both.

Strategies get talked about, thought about, praised, condemned, compared, criticised, even evaluated. But too often, the last thing they get, is done.

Whether we want to lose weight, start a business, write a book, do the Marmotte, score a goal, achieve anything, anything at all, we need to clear the blinkers, see the Destination, and get on the right route.

Then we take the first step. Then the next. And the one after that. And keep on taking them. And if we do, it's impossible not to arrive at *a* Destination.

The route, the direction, may change along the way; there'll be diversions, distractions, obstacles. The vigour, the power, we exert may vary.

There'll be the odd stone in the shoe. We take it off, shake it out, and continue. We'll trip over a rock, fall in a ditch, be given the wrong direction, get mugged, robbed, along the way.

But we keep on taking the steps.

Because of our enduring determination, we'll also get good directions, a generous lift on the back of a trailer, the odd place to stay for the night, a good meal, some warm hospitality. We'll learn to discriminate. What's good. What's not so good.

We'll learn who's lying and who's telling the truth. We'll learn when to stroll and when to sprint, when to keep a straight course and when to divert. We'll learn the weather signs, when to find shelter, when to let rip on the open road, and go for all we're worth.

But we keep the Destination in mind, always, always, always seeing it in the mind's eye. Then every tactic we contrive, every angle we consider, every delay we encounter, every step we take, will keep us on the right track, help us get there.

It's a good way to live.

A sense of Direction and a strong sense of Personal Purpose are sources of energy to a life, no matter where it may be at any given moment.

A Churchill Story....

Nearly 50 years ago, a tutor on a course I was doing, told me a story about Winston Churchill visiting his school in the early 1960's. My tutor's name was Ken, a North Yorkshire man, who not only tutored me in Sports Psychology, but how to quaff Newcastle Brown, and appreciate the less fine points of Rugby League.

Anyway, the boys of the school were to gather in the Assembly Hall, and Mr. Churchill was expected to speak for about an hour.

Ken told me that not one of the boys in the school was looking forward to listening to the ex-Prime Minister, now well into his third age, and almost forgotten, despite his illustrious past, speaking for that length of time. They had different priorities; sport, distractions, water-games, girls, comics.

On top of that, the media of the day tended to portray Churchill as a bit of a has-been, a brandy-swilling, cigar puffing megalomaniac, who was well past his sell-by date.

But the event was booked, and it went ahead. The hall was filled with chattering boys, about five hundred of them, and they were briefed by the Headmaster about giving the Guest of Honour a warm welcome.

After that, the Headmaster then introduced Sir Winston Churchill.

Churchill shambled out onto the stage, acknowledged the desultory ripple of applause that greeted him, and stood, hunched, bent, aged, in front of his slightly puzzled young audience.

For nearly a full minute, he looked, wordless, round the hall. He seemed to be searching the faces, looking for a responsive expression, maybe a curious pupil, an interested face, some young mind with which he might communicate.

Then, Ken said, he seemed to take a decision. He straightened up, threw back his shoulders, and wrapped his stick sharply on the stage floor.

In a sonorous tone charged with emotion, defiance and self-assurance, he declared, "Never!".

And he then spent another thirty seconds scanning the audience before rapping hard on the floor again, and repeating in an even harder, more commanding tone, "Never!!", pausing and letting his audience feel the weight of his gaze.

He then rapped the hard metal ferrule of the stick, for the third time, on the stage floor, and drawing himself to his full height, opened his shoulders and declared in an authoritative, forceful, stentorian command, "Never! Never! Never!..Give Up!"

As he was turning to leave the stage, and his stunned and silent audience, it was as if all the tales, all the stories, all the famous and witty quotes, and related incidents of bravery, cunning, influence, malevolence, vices and virtues, and eloquence, converged and erupted in a tumultuous, thunderous, delirious roar of cheering approval from five hundred young throats, which filled the hall for a full five minutes after the old man had left.

My tutor, Ken, who cherished the memory, was visibly moved in the telling of it.

He finished his narrative with, "And he'd achieved more in four minutes, David, than most of us could in four hours."

I relate this because I had word recently that Ken has died. I never forgot his story. I see it as a clear and vivid memory of a privileged and memorable acquaintance.

Truly, one of his life's great events. R.I.P.

Joseph's Story

Joseph is 63. He's good at what he does and has made a success of his life; family cared for, nice house, lovely part of the country, he's comfortably off.

The other day, he said, 'I wish I'd known about this 30 years ago. I'd have saved myself a lot of wear and tear.'

He has lost a good bit of fat, toned his body and restored his energy.

What Joseph discovered was that energy has a lot to do with the state of mind, and that the body must be able to do its part.

We can have many resources, great abilities, and even the opportunities to use them, but if the awareness of how to use those abilities, and the mind and body aren't in tune, access is difficult. Even impossible.

The prevailing attitude, the emotional state, the sheer physical competence, govern our ability to use what's available to us. Or not.

These aptitudes have been described, by people who should know better, as 'soft skills'. The implication is that they're 'nice things to know', pleasant conversational topics, but not necessary. If you have a few moments to spare, it's a nice way to amuse yourself.

Science, Life, and a rapidly developing awareness in the world of Personal Performance is telling a different story. I.Q., (Intelligence Quotient) used to be the measure of what your potential was.

Continuing research is showing that Emotional Intelligence (E.Q.), is, and always has been, the major factor in human development and achievement.

Decades of research at Multi-Health Systems in Toronto, Canada, and other leading research houses in the field, have shown that, on average, IQ accounts for just about 6% of our success today's entrepreneurial environment, depending on the role concerned.

EQ has been shown to account for between 27% and 45%'

Which is why it's important not just to know your stuff, but that you feel right about it too.

And that you're in a fit state to do it; Fit for Purpose.

What Can You Do ...?

Here's a question for you. What can you do with your potential?

Eh?

Stop sometime this morning. Get a pen, and a note-book.

Ask yourself, and then, more importantly, answer yourself.

What can you do about your potential? Really, truly, *do* about it?

You don't have to spend the rest of the day on it, not all at once anyhow.

But you can go back to it. And start noticing it, your potential. You can see it in all sorts of ways, how you work, how you speak, how you think, how you feel.

How you live.

It can grow gently into your life, as a quiet, determined and reliable force. It can bring tremendous power and vitality into your days.

So, go ahead. Ask.

And then answer.

Daily Decision

Every morning is the start of a new day and another step.

What gives force and energy to the day is the quality of thought and action we bring to it.

So, the start of the day is key to your potential being brought to bear.

That's when *you* decide on a good day, or a bad one.

No matter what happens, you can decide to fire on all cylinders, or not.

And that's the difference, isn't it? Every day.

So now, when you say, 'Have a good one', mean it.

Persistence...When it Doesn't Matter....

You'd wonder sometimes if persistence isn't some myth on which we all feel we need to expound ad nauseam.

Now why would anyone say that? Here's why; the need for persistence only exists when something has been

a) decided and

b) started.

There's a great deal of talk, and acres of paper used, on the value of persistence.

But persistence is dependent on those two conditions.

If the decision hasn't been taken, and nothing started, there's no need for persistence.

So, decide now, then start immediately.

And then Persist.

Learning to Get It Done......

A lot of our education is about filling our poor heads with facts and figures, memorising by rote, and passing a written exam on material most of which we'll have cast aside by the time the exam is over.

Not a lot of our education is geared on how to survive in the world, or how to communicate with our fellow man.

We hit the street, and find that the fellow who left school five years before us, at thirteen years of age, is now hiring, and if we're lucky, may take us on and put us on the road to earning a living.

Some would see that as a bit over the top and not the norm. And my take to that view would be that the viewer has been victim of the educational system. He has succumbed to the idealism that everyone goes to school, gets educated, employed, married, rears a family, lives and dies.

And yes, there are great advantages to the discipline of learning, memorising and repeating in an intelligible and ordered way that makes sense to an examiner, and it does train the mind to pay attention.

But one of the Life Skills is doing, now, what needs to be done.

And often, that's the difference between worry and peace of mind, success and failure, happiness and sorrow.

A whole industry has sprung up out of Procrastination.

Procrastination is putting off what we know we need to do, but don't want to.

And what we want, beats what we need, any day.

One solution I, and very many who've tried it, is that even if you loathe what you've got to do, get started.

Whatever chance we have of completing something we start, we've no chance of completing what hasn't even been started. And sometimes we need to restart, every day. But that's ok, isn't it?

Between the starts and finishes, in stages, it will eventually get done.

So quit stewing and start doing.

Now, breathe, and get on with it.

Great Reasons to Be Well

There are many good, even great, reasons why you should take a few simple steps to keep yourself healthy and well.

You'll live longer, have more energy, less, a lot less, distress, and you'll cope better in times of difficulty.

You'll also get more from the good times, feel better about your life, and actually contribute to the lives of those near and dear to you.

You'll be a good person to be around. People will feel better for having met you and known you.

Make the most of your personal assets, for life, for business, for sport, for personal expression, for any of the things that are important to you.

What are these assets? They're the qualities you have.

Are you persistent?

Are you imaginative? Maybe someone dismissed you as a dreamer.

Dreams need imagination.

Can you empathise with your fellow-man? That's the fabric of compassion.

Have you habits that are good, for you and for others? They were learned, just like the not-so-good habits. The fact of the good ones proves you can form them.

Are you decisive? Life is a series of decisions. Ninety percent of them are unconscious.

Start being selective in your decisions. That alone will change direction in any life.

And your life.

How do you do it?

You stay well.

Decide now to stay healthy, well and fit. Then you've a foundation for anything else you want to do.

PEP up your life.... Three Things You Need for Results...

Put regularity into any system you're practising. It doesn't matter what it is; if you don't *do* it, it doesn't get done.

The First Law for Learning is repetition.

The First Law for Arriving is taking the steps to get there, turn up. Woody Allen speaks of simply turning up being one of the most crucial factors in succeeding at anything.

Energise your application.

Do it as if you mean it. You don't have to kill yourself, but putting a bit of punch into what you do gives the body, the mind and the soul a part to play in it.

It's what the Famous Managers mean when they talk about 'spirit'. It's what we all mean when we say a team has spirit, soul, heart; it's not a physical heart that pumps blood, nor a Holy Soul that may go to Heaven or Hell.

Muhammed Ali had heart; James Brown, Aretha Franklin, Joe Dolan, had soul. They also had the Spirit of their performance. It's the essence of the man or woman doing it.

Persist. Persistence is what raises and exercises the indomitability of the Human Spirit. Persistence takes courage, belief, conviction.

They're the so-called soft skills you need to for the hard road.

Turbo-Charge Monday...

Start your week with a resounding decision. For this week, with this week only on your mind, decide to give yourself the benefit of the priceless gift of energy.

Here's how.

Decide. Decide right now that what powers of concentration, of physical health, and intended potential, that you have, will be brought to this one week in which you will shine.

Decide it right now and then begin to act on it.

Do something, anything, right now, that you've been putting off, something that just needs to be done, something that should have been done one time before, could have been done many times before, and hasn't yet been done.

Decide to do it.

Right now.

Get it done and then get on to the next thing.

And get it done.

And then the third.

That's all.

Close this book now and go get it done.

The Scourge and the Blessing of Habit...........

Habit is described in one dictionary as 'an acquired behaviour pattern regularly followed until it has become involuntary.'

An American philosopher described habit as chains, that they were 'too weak to be felt, till they're too strong to be broken'.

And we all have them. They can be changed, interrupted, improved, overcome, learned and used for both good and bad.

They tie in hugely with our fundamental beliefs about life.

Here's a little exercise; make a list , say 10, of your useful habits, and a list of 10 of the not-so useful ones.

You may be surprised and enlightened by what comes up.

Don't worry about changing them at this moment.

Just be ruthlessly honest with yourself, and note the debits as well as the credits.

For the next couple of days, review them. See what's working for you and what's working against you. Do this for 5 minutes, a couple of times a day.

Meet with yourself and scour these habits. Then after about three days, you can ask yourself if any of them might be worth changing.

The Birth of Belief...

Every cell in your body is affected by how you stand, walk, sit, carry yourself, and by what you eat and drink.

And by how you think.

When you use your posture well, have good breathing patterns, eat and drink half-way decently, you're likely to be in good shape.

Reinforce that with reasonable optimism, a positive attitude, and a forward -searching outlook, and you'll develop a strength in character, an indomitable will, and eventful, and mostly happy, life.

This isn't just some randomly pleasant idea I picked out of the sky.

Research by a Nutrition Group in the U.K., over a period of years, with over 55,000 people, found that the top 101 very healthy individuals of that group considered the following aspects to be most important in their achievement;

1. State of Mind 85%

2. Nutrition 84%

3. Exercise 93%

4. Relationship 58%

5. Spirituality 83%

Of that group, 73% thought themselves fulfilled, 71% considered themselves happy, and a huge 78% had a strong sense of Personal Purpose.

The interesting thing about Personal Purpose is that it usually reveals itself in adversity.

As individuals, and groups, we often find our best qualities when challenged in life. We dig in and find resources we never knew we had, or resurrect those we'd forgotten about, dismissed.

Which is why sometimes, when we come through a crisis, though glad to be through it, we miss the sense of urgency, the energy it brought, the feeling of being really alive, fully aware of the height to which our senses and abilities can soar.

As a simple exercise in Mind Training, get a pen and paper, a quiet spot, turn off the phone, isolate yourself, for 5 minutes.

Now, to the exclusion of anything else, write only on one difficulty you've overcome, at some time in your life. Note the qualities you brought to it.

Write in detail how you felt, what you thought, what the weather was like, what you wore, the moments of doubt you had to force yourself through, the sense of will, determination, that bore you through the shaky moments, the realisation that you could do it, and come out at the other end.

No short cutting.

5 minutes.

Stop the world.

Live in this. Face it.

Write till to the 60th second of the fifth minute.

Finish it.

The Power of Adversity............

The last piece indicated how the body is affected by thought. From what I've heard over the years, I think we're all well agreed on that.

The mind plays a large part in the condition and function of the body. And it's been researched to the ends of the earth, so that science now supports a lot of the ideas that everyone believed in.

In the world of personal Health and Fitness, this has been shown to have amazing effects. Not only have people managed their minds to cope with life-altering circumstances but opened channels of possibility and recuperation that otherwise would never have existed.

But this can be seen every weekend in the sporting world. Watch the body language of players go through the full range of performance from dithering hesitation to powerful achievement, and back again, in the space of 70-80 minutes.

And the same goes for life. We can run from despair to victorious triumph in a matter of weeks, days, or even hours.

This is usually a reflection of the prevailing attitude of the person concerned. Speaking of attitude, I recently had the privilege of a long talk with a man who is terminally ill. While the attitude was one of acceptance, he also had what I would call a realistic and understandable anger, not a begrudging kind for others healthier, but at being, as he put it, 'hauled off the pitch before the game was over'.

He said he'd be having words with his Maker. He felt cheated, but, oddly, not resentful.

He behaved with the kind of bravery that one reads about in the prison camps, the disasters, the accidents and events that turn lives upside down and bring seismic change. While there was the humility of acceptance, there was also the energy of deprivation. And no self-pity.

For many days afterwards, I had that feeling of having had an experience I couldn't quite define.

What's coming now, I think, is a recognition of an example of quiet, determined and indomitable courage.

An unostentatious example, it reflected the attitude with which I've always associated him.

May we be grateful.

And, Fitness for the Brain......

In response to enquiries about Mental Fitness, this piece will give pointers on how to nourish the brain cells, train the mind, and make the most of mental energy.

Nourishment first. A great deal of the food eaten today is so deficient in vitamin, mineral and trace content, that you'd wonder if it shouldn't be called something else.

'Food-Replacement', 'Eating-Bulk,' 'Stomach-Filler', come to mind as appropriate descriptions.

Brain cells, just like the cells that make up everything else, need nourishment. We should get this from what we eat. But we don't. We get, consequently, confusion, depression, poor concentration.

If the right ingredients aren't in the recipe, you can cook how you like; you won't get the cake you hoped for.

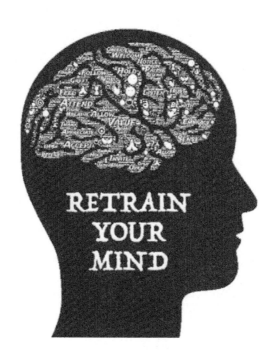

RETRAIN YOUR MIND

You need vitamins, minerals, trace elements and protein. You need a small amount of sugars, starches, and a little bit of fat in the body too.

Most of the Western diet today is full of sugar, starch and fat, with a little bit of a vitamin or mineral supplement thrown in to validate it as a food.

And we end up being overfed, undernourished and overweight.

So, *what can* you do? *How can* you make the most of your food, get the best benefits, and live a normal life? (Do those questions ring a bell?)

Well, try this for a start. But only try it if you're going to be a bit earnest about it. It's not for you if you don't intend to do it with a bit of a will, a bit of determination. Do it as if you mean it.

To create a truly positive effect on the body, including the brain cells, try the following suggestion.

Do it for a week.

Cut your sugar containing foods RIGHT DOWN. And the starches, bread, pasta, biscuits, chocolatey snacks, ices.

Eat at mealtimes only, unless you've a dietary condition.

Use eggs, fish, poultry, lean meats. CHEW them. Use vegetable or salads to supplement them.

Have the occasional treat of a small dessert.

If you don't think you're getting enough nutrients, use a supplement. Ask your chemist or Health Food Store to advise you. Any of the Brand names are good.

If you really get waspish or ratty because you're low on sugar, use a fruit. Drink water. Try it slightly warmed, body temperature.

On paper this looks really simple, and so it is. But we're so ingrained with habit that it can contrive to seem difficult.

Which is where the other nourishment comes in; the Mindforce.

Start this with a resolute decision. That's your first step. Decide and do.

Have a great day, and travel safely.

Climb the Mountain, Walk the Walk, and Swim With the Sharks...

There's a trend today to travel to named places. Many visit Everest stay around the bottom, or go to one of the base camps. Some walk the Camino in Northern Spain.

Others go to the Caribbean and swim with sharks

As far as I can see, by witnessing the place in which some climber, saint, or explorer experienced his deliverance, we can hope to absorb some of his qualities

Not a bad idea.

I once went to see Francis Chichester's Gypsy Moth in Greenwich. I felt inspired by looking, just looking, at that tiny vessel in which he'd circumnavigated the oceans of the world, through storms, hurricanes, and mountainous seas, to arrive back to the South Coast of England in one piece, man and boat. And all done single-handedly.

I was reminded of these kinds of challenges recently. What triggered it was the chance meeting of an old pal whom I hadn't seen in just on 50 years. We met as the two of us were visiting our respective parents' graves in St. Ibar's cemetery, or Crosstown, in Wexford.

I'll call him Jimmy.

We'd first met in our late teens. Jimmy hadn't been as selective as I'd been in his choice of parents, and had come up through a background of poverty, hardship and wanton violence. He was a tough kid, resilient and brave.

As far as Jimmy was concerned, his weakness was that he had a kind heart. It endeared him to many people, me included. As youngsters, we both had musical aspirations. We had encouraged each other in our efforts. I was half-way serious about what I wanted to achieve.

But nowhere as serious as Jimmy.

Jimmy burned. His desire scorched hours into his days, energy into his hours, persistent focus into his actions. And he had an indomitable belief.

All this was exemplified in his decision to quit school, in the year of his Leaving Cert, in which he stood to do well, join a show band, and go on the road.

Not too long after he'd done this, the showband scene began to wane, giving way to the rock groups and Folk movement, and as many of the bands became redundant, most of the musicians went back to their day jobs.

Not Jimmy, though.

He kept practising his trumpet, studying musical theory and learning about other aspects of showbusiness. When the showband scene finally folded, Jimmy went to London, played with commercial dance bands, got into session work, and regularly played small jazz venues for his own enjoyment and musical development.

Then came the car crash. After the fourth or fifth operation, he was left with two nerve-damaged right-hand fingers, a nearly new mouth, new teeth, and no embouchure to speak of.

Not good for a trumpet player.

He could, just about, coax some strangulated noises from his beloved instrument. So, he started teaching, became one of the best in that business, and meanwhile continued his musical theory study. He submitted projects and achieved success in the film music industry. He then financed and set up a musical instrument shop in Soho, having it run by two fellow musicians who were good teachers and good salespeople.

For four years, the shop sold more in a week than many shops sold in months. Jimmy was beginning to think in terms of semi-retirement and devoting his time to full-time screen writing.

Then one day the shop didn't open, and Jimmy was called. His partners had disappeared and so had Jimmy's money. All of it. Huge debts had accumulated.

Apart from the financial implosion, Jimmy was truly devastated by the betrayal. And it wasn't just by his ex-partners. His wife had gone off with one of them, leaving two bewildered children with him.

He says they were what saved him.

By this time, he had re-educated his mouth and lips to blow a trumpet, and the other right hand fingers to negotiate the valves. Now in his late thirties, he was back on the road, and getting radio, TV and film work again.

Slowly, doggedly, he kept to his purpose, month by month, year by year, and not only negotiated discounts on otherwise impossible debt, but put the children through school and college, and years later, in his late forties, found himself debt-free, sane, and sound.

Teaching again, and playing, and getting back into writing, with some success, he was experiencing a modicum of comfort.

When the cancer hit.

For three years he endured treatment, crippling doubt, but from somewhere, summoned the courage and will and the belief to persist.

Good health eventually prevailed, and he continued his battle with life and living, collecting an Honorary Doctorate from an American University School of Music en route.

I listened to his story, told with gratitude for having been able to give his children comfort, a sense of self-belief, and an enthusiasm for their lives. And he was enjoying some comfort too, with a new woman, at the onset of third age.

Jimmy had never been to Everest. Nor had he ever done a long walk in Northern Spain. And he had only a vague notion of, and less interest in, the Caribbean.

But he had climbed his mountains, walked his walk, and swum with the worst kind of sharks.

We parted with the usual sincere promises to keep in touch. Maybe we will. I certainly hope so.

And I was left with a reinforced thought that it isn't what happens to us in life, but how we respond to it, that so often makes us or breaks us. And further, whatever circumstance we find ourselves in, we always, always, always, have the choice to bring the best of who we are, where we are, with what we've got, to bear on it.

The Right Question............

When the distasteful substance hits the fan, we often instinctively ask ourselves, 'Why does this always happen to me?', or 'How did I get myself into this?', or 'Can't I do *anything* right?'.

Look at those questions. Look at them.

And what do you hear?

You'll be hearing the sort of answers that won't be helpful. At all.

Those questions trigger the mind to dredge up the self-deprecating kind of answer that's going to put you into a downward spiral self-ridicule, sabotage and ultimately despair and depression.

And it's so fast, you won't even realise what you're doing to yourself.

A lot of people practise self-effacement as a way of being humble. You'll hear it nearly every time you pay someone a compliment. The sports stars talk of being at the right place at the right time, implying the huge luck that put them there.

The lady who gets a compliment on her outfit, or some other aspect of appearance, will often dismiss it with the statement that it was the only one left, or that she bought it by mistake, but it didn't turn out too badly.

When people make a mistake, they can either try to cover it up, deny it, or dig a grave of deep remorse and self-belittlement.

Now, responsibility is good. If we make a mistake, do wrong, offend someone, we need to be big enough to admit to it, make our apologies, and then do whatever we can to right what wrong exists.

Which is what the questioning is about. Try, *'How can* I fix this?', *How can I* cope with this'

You'll be sending your mind in a better direction.

You'll be searching for a solution. You'll feel better, a hell of a lot better, and you'll be dealing and living in the realm of possibility.

And just because you may not see a way through just yet, stick with it.

Your brain will be working away at it, chipping away, collecting and discarding alternatives and building knowledge on how to deal with the challenge. So, persist.

As an example, *how can you* make this a great day?

And have a great day.

Fit for Purpose??

A telling phrase, isn't it, 'Fit for Purpose.'

There are people in the world with the qualities of talent, intelligence, diligence, courage, and yet, find that they're living their lives like square pegs in round holes. Many of the people so afflicted would not be aware that that's what's wrong in the first place.

We can be so conditioned to the notion of what constitutes success that we may not realise our dilemma. So, we can't fix it.

Which is why it's often a good idea to look at ourselves, and our lives. Often. To take the time, to evaluate what we're doing, where we are, where we might want to go, how we might get there, what it is that gives meaning, direction a sense of purpose to us, as individuals.

And after all that, maybe to realise that where we are isn't so bad after all. And that's the beauty of our personal liberty, to be able to choose.

We don't have to drop everything, abandon life as we know it, run out to Ryanair and lose ourselves on a distant beach where we can contemplate the mysteries of life and be at one with ourselves. We can do that anywhere.

And it's good to know that a sense of purpose can be found anywhere, rediscovered at any time, resurrected at will, at any time in our lives, should we choose to look for it.

Nor does it have change the world, right all wrongs, or even make a difference.

Any sense of purpose, a real one, is what gives direction and meaning to anyone. And it's his business, no one else's. So long as it doesn't harm or encroach on another, it can be whatever it is. What does it for you? What might reinforce, or, for that matter, *bring* that kind of force to your life? Or refresh it?

Take the time. Give it a bit of consideration. Let it swim round in your head, pleasantly. No rush. You don't have to hit a deadline, make a target, prove anything. This is a pleasant exercise for relaxing, refreshing and recharging the mind. Enjoy it.

Have a good weekend, drive safely, drink wisely.

Now, there's a thought.

Fit for What?

Most people with whom I work, and who follow the programme, get pleasant surprises.

They're surprises because they weren't really expected.

For example, one man gets up earlier every morning, gets his administration done and out of the way by 9am. From 9 am onwards, it's all productive business.

A self-employed lady, a sole trader, does the same. The formula self-perpetuates.

Morning efficiency, frequently done, fires a self-belief, a feeling of competence, which burgeons into a surge of productive activity.

This lays the foundation, a basis, a kick start to the day.

And all this came from one perception; *they had a look at themselves, what they were doing, what they were producing, and decided to make a change.*

What they saw was that YOU are the epicenter of your operation. YOU are at the helm.

If you're not happy at how your ship is navigating the sea of performance, look at the Captain.

Have a word, a meeting, with him.

Is he fit for purpose?

That's where it starts. And ends.

Copy that question into your diary. Mull over it.

Frequently.

Your Choice

'It isn't what the book, product, course, service, consultation costs. It's what the cost of *not* availing yourself of it that can matter.'

"What we ponder and what we think about sets the course of our life. Any day we wish; we can discipline ourselves to change it all.

Any day we wish, we can open the book that will open our mind to new knowledge.

Any day we wish, we can start a new activity.

Any day we wish, we can start the process of life change. We can do it immediately, or next week, or next month, or next year.

"We can also do nothing. We can pretend rather than perform. And if the idea of having to change ourselves makes us uncomfortable, we can remain as we are. We can choose rest over labor, entertainment over education, delusion over truth, and doubt over confidence.

The choices are ours to make.

But while we curse the effect, we continue to nourish the cause. As Shakespeare uniquely observed, "The fault is not in the stars, but in ourselves."

We created our current circumstances by our past choices.

We have both the ability and the responsibility to make better choices, beginning today.

A Terrible, Terrible Thing...

Wouldn't it be a terrible thing, a truly terrible thing, to reach your own imagined age of expiry, full of regret, remorse and sadness?

Many, sadly, arrive at that time of life to the accompaniment of the words, 'If only....'

That need never be.

No matter what the circumstances are, and I was relating to a gentleman just the other day how I'm regularly inspired by people, many of whom have suffered huge losses, financially, personally, emotionally, and how they deal with those events in their lives. They always find some way of coping.

You'll never read about them in the papers, hear them on the radio, see them on TV. But they're there, in their thousands, making the most of who they are, where they are, with what they've got.

What they show is that you can decide, at any time, to regroup, resolve and recapture the energy and vitality of life.

On that note, have a great weekend

Heavy Breathing, Sex, and You..........

Breathing is important for living longer.

It helps your mood and keeps you performing at your best. Look at some benefits of deep breathing.

1. Breathing Detoxifies and Releases Toxins

Your body is designed to release much of its generated toxins through breathing. If you are *not* breathing effectively, you're *just not* ridding your body of toxins, wastes, poisons.

Which is one of the reasons you'll rarely see an athlete with pimples.

Heavy breathing does the trick.

If you can't get conventional exercise, talk to your partner. Make some dates.

Arrange some heavy breathing sessions.

2. Breathing Releases Tension

Think how your body feels when you are tense, angry, scared or stressed.

It constricts.

The body gets tight and can't function.

Get breathing. Whatever kind of exercise does it for you, get at it.

Long Ago, Before the Self-Help Explosion...

Do you remember Richard Harris, the wonderful Limerick born actor who shot to fame in the film, 'This Sporting Life'?

While I admired Harris, I thought even more of the man who wrote that gritty, realistic, yet touching novel, David Storey.

Using his own experience as an example, it was said that he gave great support and encouragement to the relatively new cast of actors in the film, which was then a controversial groundbreaker for the film industry.

His advice to himself, and to others, was encapsulated in the idea that when you achieve one thing well, big or small, you can achieve another.

This, he often said, was how he got through novels, plays, film scripts, the number of which he completed being prolific.

Many of them were of a new genre, not only requiring the necessary skills, assuredness, and talent of a professional writer, but immense belief in the value of them, and no small amount of courage.

But the principle applies to anything, doesn't it?

A Wise Bit of Nonsense...

Whatever your core function is, apply yourself to it. That's what gets success, achieves what you set out to do.

It's the result of applying simple means, ordinary powers, with extraordinary persistence, that knocks down walls, opens doors, wears down the opposing thoughts within us.

The humorist John Billings had a good take on this when he extolled the qualities of a postage stamp.

'It serves us all well,' he observed, 'to see how a little item like that sticks with the one thing, no matter how long or arduous the journey, till it gets there'.

The Freedom of Discipline...

How do we know when we've taken a decision?

When we take a real decision, there's a certainty to life.

It liberates the mind from doubt and procrastination.

It also tends to free us from distraction.

Sometimes we think we've decided something when we haven't; we've just made a wish.

We know the decision's been made when we find ourselves *doing something differently;* getting up a bit earlier, or not eating that muffin, or going straight home on a Friday night, not calling at the lounge bar, or being pleasant to someone we'd rather not, or finishing something when we'd rather be watching the game, or fulfilling a promise when we don't really want to.

That's decisiveness. That's freedom. It's the liberation that discipline gives us.

Ambush!

One of the best ways of getting something done is to ambush yourself.

Do this as an exercise to get your day into gear, the revs high, and watch yourself eat up the miles of work that can otherwise seem overwhelming.

Make an agreement with yourself the night before. Write it out. Plan it. Execute it.

Say you want to get up early in the morning, and make some notes to set your day in ordered motion,

Write, the night before, 'Out of bed, 6 am.' Write it, put it beside your bed, and when your alarm goes off, your obedient subconscious kicks into action, you'll awaken, and without thinking, get moving.

Don't hesitate for a split second; the decision's been taken, you're responding to your directive. Keep it going.

And then get working on the project that you've committed to and keep on doing it.

Do NOT hesitate. Keep going till it's finished, done, complete.

And you'll be amazed at the number of tasks you'll undertake, put in your list, and get done.

The biggest single factor in procrastination is thinking.

When we overthink, we give ourselves all the reasons why the project won't work.

That doesn't mean we slalom into everything that suggests itself to us. That's why you get it decided the night before; then the considerations have been viewed, the disadvantages dealt with, and the possibilities seen.

So, having taken the decision, the only thing preventing it being done is..................?

You're right; doing it, acting.

So, give your life a lift. Examine some of those brilliant ideas that flit in and out of your mind at odd times, and this time, instead of giving it the long finger, take a decision on it.

And honour your decision.

What's Your Story....?

I asked a pal of mine recently who his favourite thriller writer was.

'Elmore Leonard, Peter Cheney, and William Shakespeare', he answered.

He went on to say that in his view the best writers told a great story, that there were a few basic plots into which every story fell, even if it wasn't planned by the author. Just a few.

It didn't matter who the story was about, where it took place, when it happened, they all fell into those few plots.

He went on to say that the best stories are usually biographical, as they have a ring of truth about them, elements of reality to which the author can relate and the reader can identify.

Good novelists, he added, have an imagination that allows them to live the experiences about which they're writing, and thus bring a sense of realism and truth to their work.

Which got me to thinking; what's my story?

And, I ask, what's yours? You can have some fun and discovery with this.

Maybe it'd be good for all of us now and again to ask ourselves, 'What's my story?'

How am I living it?

Am I following a plot? A good one? A poor one? A conclusive one? A dangerous one? A pointless one? A useful one? One with a purpose?

Here's an interesting question; will it have a happy ending?

Or, will I feel, when I'm 95, did I follow the plan? Play my game? Did I even have a plan?

And, one more question; *How can I pull a plan into place, see it, and put it into practice?*

And that's the great thing about being human, isn't it, we can make, relate and live, any plan we choose.

And write our own lives. At any time in our lives.

Of course, it's not quite as simple as that, **but it's a good place to start.**

How to Have a Great Day...

In an instant, life can change.

An event, an insight, a word, can change our perception. This works both ways; for us, and against us.

We can be plummeted into misery, or we can be uplifted, exalted, inspired. We need to be aware of one thing, and that is *that we influence* which way we go.

What we intend, what we constantly think about, and how we think about it, tends to become.

Mindful Awareness is seeing how we think. The greatest achievements started somewhere as an idea in someone's mind. So did the greatest calamities.

By being mindful of our thoughts, watching them, we can begin to direct them to what we wish to become, to achieve, to have.

Constant attention to an idea, or aspiration, or skill or craft, allows us insights and revelations that are not available to the inattentive mind. That may seem obvious, but it's an obvious that often hides in obscurity.

Most of our thinking is reactionary. By deciding to think *proactively* about something that we wish to accomplish, we alter our thinking, our perceptions, and how we feel and particularly how we behave towards that goal.

The effects of active thinking direct our attention. Our attention, applied to what we intend, drives our feelings and our behaviour.

This is how a Statement of Intent can influence our lives. It's a declaration.

When we articulate an idea into a statement, we crystallise it in our minds and direct our attention.

With attention, our minds become clearer, more familiar with it. It starts to become an aim for us to pursue. Life has meaning. It influences how we think, what we do, how we use ourselves in life. That creates direction.

And that's what is generally known as a sense of purpose.

It goes for *any pursuit, any circumstance, any life.*

Life Force...

It's generally held that the average person achieves peak lung function in their mid-twenties.

Then they begin to lose lung capacity, not from illness or disease, but from disuse. Therefore some people *arrive at the age of 60 with about 50% of their lung capacity.*

Diminished lung capacity means shallow breathing, rapid breathing, inadequate oxygenation of the body. It means tension, poor circulation, fatigue and confusion.

Health suffers. Spirit declines. Illness flourishes. Life shortens.

And these effects are unnecessary.

Unless breathing capacity is actively used, it diminishes. As the saying goes, 'Use it or lose it'.'

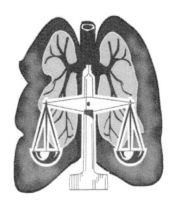

Exercise alone *helps*; but to **ensure***full active lung capacity,* we need *to specifically train the breathing apparatus.* That's what fundamental breathing practice is about.

Learn the skill. Practice it. Then get good at it.

Maintain healthy lungs.

Protect your health.

Raise your spirit.

Live long.

What're Your Intentions...?

Whatever you give your attention to, gets energy from you, and it grows.

Be clear on this.

This is not some fluffy notion gleaned from the back cover of some current Guru's Self-Help tome.

Every effect has a cause. It's one of Nature's laws.

Everything that has come about in the march of human existence has been the result of intention, attention, followed by action.

Some people have great intentions, ideas, but don't attend to the plan, the development, the means to bringing it about. Others have great ideas and intentions, plan it to the Nth degree, then stick it in a drawer or the filing cabinet and forget about it. They take no action, for any number of reasons.

Others get an idea, sketch the plan on the back of an envelope in the pub or the coffee shop, and then get to it, moving anybody and anything that will help the execution of the plan.

And even though the idea is new and untested, the plan may be a sketch of the idea, they take the all-important step of *doing* it.

Their intention is now the object of their attention, and the attention is on the action.

So, there it is for any idea; business, the arts, personal, weight loss, a course in some fondly thought-of subject; anything, anything at all.

Figure out what you intend. Attend to the next step. And go and do it.

Sunday Night and You Feel Like...

It's Sunday night

And you're not quite right,

And Monday's in the warning.

But how the hell

Can you feel well,

And be up and about in the morning?

So, do be wise,

And exercise,

You'll soon be feeling better.

You'll quickly see,

How you can be

A morning-time go-getter.

And that's the trick,

When you're feeling sick

In the evening on a Sunday.

Decide instead

To use your head,

And brighten up your Monday.

Extraordinary Application.

It's over 50 years ago, now. We were approaching the Easter holidays, and my mom asked me what I was going to do about my Leaving Exam. With about 7 weeks, or just over, to go to the exam, I hadn't much of an answer.

I was good at Latin and English, because I enjoyed them. But the other subjects were a nuisance; something to be endured, or preferably avoided, while I attended to important matters like listening to the Stan Kenton Band, Gerry Mulligan, Billie Holiday, Ella Fitzgerald, and my hero at that time, Gene Krupa.

If those names mean nothing to you, they were a tiny few of the musicians around whom my world circled. Such was my interest in nearly all kinds of Jazz, that if I wasn't listening to it, talking about it, or thinking of it in some form, I considered the time being wasted.

So, back to my mom's question; what was I going to do about my leaving cert? For an hour or two, the question hung idly in my mind. I wasn't really concerned. And then, a shiver of alarm ran through me.

I realized, that on the amount of study to which I'd applied myself, up to that moment, my chances of passing an exam in any of the subjects other than the two I've mentioned, amounted to very, very, little.

Dread seeped through me. Fear, fanned by a creative imagination, caught light and flamed into something approaching an emotional conflagration.

It was as if the continuous barrage of parental invective over the year was suddenly accumulating into a pointed, gathering force that was hell bent on swamping me in a tsunami of guilt, fear, uncertainty and self-doubt.

To this day, I can hear my mother's sad and frequent laments; 'What in God's name is the matter with you?', 'What *are* you going to do?', 'Why can't you be like everyone else?', 'I don't know what'll become of you!', and, in times of severe distress, 'Where did I go wrong?'

I thank whoever my God is that I'd always had the wit to see that this was a rhetorical question and so I refrained from any kind of answer.

As this new experience was threatening to suck what energy there was from my existence, I realized I'd wandered, without thinking, up to the attic in the top of the house. Up here, I felt less threatened, less vulnerable, had the incipient nudges of normality returning. And this was my good luck, as I was about to read something that could so easily have been scanned, vaguely understood, and promptly dismissed.

And another thing kept the butterflies in my stomach flying in order, and that was the fact that I'd never intended not to study. I'd always been in accord with the idea of getting a good result in the Leaving Exam. But apart from the Latin and English, I'd just never got around to burdening myself with the ritual of application to any other subjects.

The attic in our house in those days was, to me, a wonderful place. On the fifth floor, it had a broad window in the roof which looked out across the town, to the river Slaney, set between the tower of Selskar Abbey and the top of the pear tree in the corner of our garden.

307

The wall at one end of the room was covered top to bottom by bookshelves, each shelf full to the edge. I was browsing through the rows of old cloth-bound books, taking out one at a time, sniffing here and there that fausty old smell that is peculiar to aged books, when I came upon one with an inscription on the second page.

The writing was in faded, sepia tinted ink, copperplate style, slanting to the right. 'From P.B. H., to P. B. H. October, 1914', it said. I knew those initials. They were my late father's. He would have been twenty in 1914, three years older than I was now.

He'd died in 1950, twelve years previously, aged 56, after a life of toil, effort, long days and hours, and I'm very pleased to say, some notable success.

Flicking through the book, a heavily underlined paragraph arrested my attention. The words underlined read, *'The greatest things in daily life are achieved, not so much by the extraordinary powers of genius and intellect, so much as by* the extraordinary application of simple means, and ordinary powers, with which we're all more or less endowed'

I read it again. And again. And then again. And yet again. I kept on reading it, over and over. Then I found myself saying it, out loud, as I was reading it. Then I found I was saying it without having to look at the words, as the idea, the truth of it, began to take hold and imprint itself on my eagerly assimilating, hungry young mind. It was growing on me. Then in me. The idea and the fact of the words were taking shape in me. They were becoming my truth.

'Extraordinary application'. How simple. What a revelation.

That's all it took. To do anything. Extraordinary application.

And I knew, I really knew, that I could, should I wish, apply myself extraordinarily. That was all it took. Extraordinary application.

I read the underlined words again.

I had seven weeks, and a few days. About sixty days altogether. And nights. I needed five subjects, including the dreaded compulsory Irish. I had two in which I knew I could do well, even excel. All I needed was three more, and I'd probably pass the Leaving. If I could pass the Leaving, I knew I would exonerate myself of the laziness that had come to represent me in most peoples' minds. But more attractive to me was the prospect of confounding those who knew me, who had come to despair of me, and ultimately, I reluctantly admitted, dismiss me.

I started that very evening. And continued. Day in, day out. And most of the nights.

I swotted, studied, revised and recited. I beamed onto everything concerning the subjects needed. Nothing else.

I became a mental magnet for anything related to those subjects. My reticular activating system kicked in and sucked up relevant details, dismissed the irrelevant.

On it went, day and night. Twenty-four hours a day, seven days a week. Sleep was brief, irregular, deep and refreshing.

The concentration was fierce, but soon levelled out at a constant and all absorbing rate, drawing in facts and figures and perceptions and retaining them with a simple clarity. The energy perpetuated itself, boundless in its awareness of what could be, was being, achieved.

I never let up.

My poor confused mother, previously critical of my indolence, now fussed and worried over me, as I read, studied, wrote and applied myself in this frenzy of academic endeavour.

But I was taking it all in my stride. I knew, I just knew, that all that I was doing was what I, or anyone for that matter, could do when necessary.

Extraordinary application. That's all it was. A flurried show of extraordinary application.

Time flies when you're that busy. The Leaving came.

And it went.

Later that summer, lodging in London, I got the results in the post.

I'd passed.

My mother wrote at length in surprise and pleasure. It was the talk of her acquaintances. Maybe, just maybe, they suggested, there was hope for me yet.

I heard about other boys, expected to do very well, who hadn't, and some of them would have to repeat.

Some of them asked me how I'd managed to pass.

'Two words', I'd answered.

'Extraordinary application.'

Printed in Great Britain
by Amazon

75104038R00190